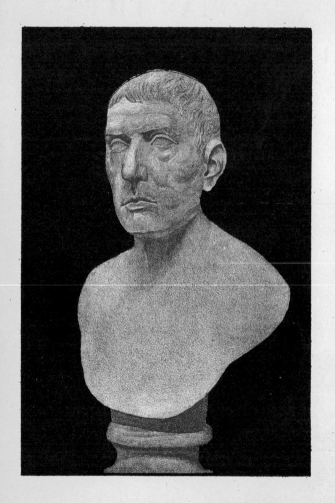

Marcus Tullius Cicero.

ROMAN LIFE
IN THE DAYS OF CICERO

SKETCHES DRAWN

FROM HIS LETTERS AND SPEECHES

BY THE

REV. ALFRED J. CHURCH, M.A.

Professor of Latin at University College, London

WITH ILLUSTRATIONS

NEW YORK

DODD, MEAD & COMPANY

PUBLISHERS

TO

OCTAVIUS OGLE,

IN REMEMBRANCE OF A LONG FRIENDSHIP,

THIS BOOK IS DEDICATED.

LIST OF ILLUSTRATIONS.

CONTENTS.

PREFACE.

THIS book does not claim to be a life of Cicero
or a history of the last days of the Roman
Republic. Still less does it pretend to come
into comparison with such a work as Bek-
ker's *Gallus*, in which on a slender thread of
narrative is hung a vast amount of facts re-
lating to the social life of the Romans. I have
tried to group round the central figure of Cicero
various sketches of men and manners, and so
to give my readers some idea of what life
actually was in Rome, and the provinces of
Rome, during the first six decades—to speak
roughly—of the first century B.C. I speak of
Cicero as the "central figure," not as judging
him to be the most important man of the time,

but because it is from him, from his speeches and
letters, that we chiefly derive the information
of which I have here made use. Hence it follows
that I give, not indeed a life of the great orator,
but a sketch of his personality and career. I have
been obliged also to trespass on the domain of
history : speaking of Cicero, I was obliged to
speak also of Cæsar and of Pompey, of Cato and
of Antony, and to give a narrative, which I have
striven to make as brief as possible, of their
military achievements and political action.   I
must apologize for seeming to speak dog-
matically on some questions which have been
much disputed. It would have been obviously
inconsistent with the character of the book to
give the opposing arguments ; and my only
course was to state simply conclusions which I
had done my best to make correct.

I have to acknowledge my obligations to Mar-
quardt's *Privat-Leben der Romer*, Mr. Capes'
University Life in Ancient Athens, and Mr.
Watson's *Select Letters of Cicero*. I have also
made frequent use of Mr. Anthony Trollope's

Life of Cicero, a work full of sound sense, though curiously deficient in scholarship.

The publishers and myself hope that the illustrations, giving as there is good reason to believe they do the veritable likenesses of some of the chief actors in the scenes described, will have a special interest. It is not till we come down to comparatively recent times that we find art again lending the same aid to the understanding of history.

Some apology should perhaps be made for retaining the popular title of one of the illustrations. The learned are, we believe, agreed that the statue known as the " Dying Gladiator" does not represent a gladiator at all. Yet it seemed pedantic, in view of Byron's famous description, to let it appear under any other name.

ALFRED CHURCH.

HADLEY GREEN
October 8, 1883.

ROMAN LIFE
IN THE DAYS OF CICERO.

———

CHAPTER I.

A ROMAN BOY.

A ROMAN father's first duty to his boy, after
lifting him up in his arms in token that he was
a true son of the house, was to furnish him with
a first name out of the scanty list (just seventeen) to which his choice was limited. This
naming was done on the eighth day after birth,
and was accompanied with some religious cere-
monies, and with a feast to which kinsfolk
were invited. Thus named he was enrolled in
some family or state register. The next care was
to protect him from the malignant influence of
the evil eye by hanging round his neck a gilded
bulla, a round plate of metal. (The *bulla* was of
leather if he was not of gentle birth.) This he
wore till he assumed the dress of manhood.

Then he laid it aside, possibly to assume it once more, if he attained the crowning honor to which a Roman could aspire, and was drawn in triumph up the slope of the Capitol. He was nursed by his mother, or, in any case, by a free-born woman. It was his mother that had exclusive charge of him for the first seven years of his life, and had much to say to the ordering of his life afterwards. For Roman mothers were not shut up like their sisters in Greece, but played no small part in affairs—witness the histories or legends (for it matters not for this purpose whether they are fact or fiction) of the Sabine wives, of Tullia, who stirred up her husband to seize a throne, or Veturia, who turned her son Coriolanus from his purpose of besieging Rome. At seven began the education which was to make him a citizen and a soldier. Swimming, riding, throwing the javelin developed his strength of body. He learned at the same time to be frugal, temperate in eating and drinking, modest and seemly in behavior, reverent to his elders, obedient to authority at home and abroad, and above all, pious towards the gods. If it was the duty of

the father to act as priest in some temple of the
State (for the priests were not a class apart from
their fellow-citizens), or to conduct the worship
in some chapel of the family, the lad would act
as *camillus* or acolyte.   When the clients, the
dependents of the house, trooped into the hall
in the early morning hours to pay their respects
to their patron, or to ask his advice and assistance in their affairs, the lad would stand by his
father's chair and make acqaintance with his
humble friends.   When the hall was thrown
open, and high festival was held, he would be
present and hear the talk on public affairs or on
past times.   He would listen to and sometimes
take part in the songs which celebrated great
heroes.   When the body of some famous soldier
or statesman was carried outside the walls to be
buried or burned, he would be taken to hear the
oration pronounced over the bier.

At one time it was the custom, if we may
believe a quaint story which one of the Roman
writers tells us, for the senators to introduce
their young sons to the sittings of their assembly, very much in the same way as the boys
of Westminster School are admitted to hear the

debates in the Houses of Parliament. The story professes to show how it was that one of the families of the race of Papirius came to bear the name of *Prætextatus, i.e.*, clad in the *prætexta* (the garb of boyhood), and it runs thus :—" It was the custom in the early days of the Roman State that the senators should bring their young sons into the Senate to the end that they might learn in their early days how great affairs of the commonwealth were managed. And that no harm should ensue to the city, it was strictly enjoined upon the lads that they should not say aught of the things which they had heard within the House. It happened on a day that the Senate, after long debate upon a certain matter, adjourned the thing to the morrow. Hereupon the son of a certain senator, named Papirius, was much importuned by his mother to tell the matter which had been thus painfully debated. And when the lad, remembering the command which had been laid upon him that he should be silent about such matters, refused to tell it, the woman besought him to speak more urgently, till at the last, being worn out by her importunities, he contrived this thing. 'The

Senate,' he said, ' debated whether something might not be done whereby there should be more harmony in families than is now seen to be ; and whether, should it be judged expedient to make any change, this should be to order that a husband should have many wives, or a wife should have more husbands than one.' Then the woman, being much disturbed by the thing which she had heard, hastened to all the matrons of her acquaintance, and stirred them up not to suffer any such thing. Thus it came to pass that the Senate, meeting the next day, were astonished beyond measure to see a great multitude of women gathered together at the doors, who besought them not to make any change ; or, if any, certainly not to permit that a man should have more wives than one. Then the young Papirius told the story how his mother had questioned him, and how he had devised this story to escape from her importunity. Thereupon the Senate, judging that all boys might not have the same constancy and wit, and that the State might suffer damage from the revealing of things that had best be kept secret, made this law, that no sons of a senator should thereafter come into the House, save only this young Papirius, but that he should have the right to come so long as he should wear the *prætexta*."

While this general education was going on, the lad was receiving some definite teaching. He learned of course to read, to write, and to cypher. The elder Cato used to write in large characters for the benefit of his sons portions of history, probably composed by himself or by his contemporary Fabius, surnamed the " Painter " (the author of a chronicle of Italy from the landing of Æneas down to the end of the Second Punic War). He was tempted to learn by playthings, which ingeniously combined instruction and amusement. Ivory letters— probably in earlier times a less costly material was used—were put into his hands, just as they are put into the hands of children now-a-days, that he might learn how to form words. As soon as reading was acquired, be began to learn by heart. " When we were boys," Cicero represents himself as saying to his brother Quintus, in one of his Dialogues, " we used to learn the ' Twelve Tables.' " The " Twelve Tables "

were the laws which Appius of evil fame and
his colleagues the decemvirs had arranged in
a code. " No one," he goes on to say, "learns
them now." Books had become far more common in the forty years which had passed between Cicero's boyhood and the time at which
he is supposed to be speaking ; and the tedious lesson of his early days had given place to
something more varied and interesting.

Writing the boy learned by following with the
pen (a sharp-pointed *stylus* of metal), forms of
letters which had been engraved on tablets of
wood. At first his hand was held and guided
by the teacher. This was judged by the ex-
perienced to be a better plan than allowing him
to shape letters for himself on the wax-covered
tablet. Of course parchment and paper were
far too expensive materials to be used for exercises and copies. As books were rare and
costly, dictation became a matter of much
importance. The boy wrote, in part at least,
his own schoolbooks. Horace remembers with
a shudder what he had himself written at the
dictation of his schoolmaster, who was accustomed to enforce good writing and spelling

with many blows. He never could reconcile himself to the early poets whose verse had furnished the matter of these lessons.

Our Roman boy must have found arithmetic a more troublesome thing than the figures now in use (for which we cannot be too thankful to the Arabs their inventors) have made it. It is difficult to imagine how any thing like a long sum in multiplication or division could have been done with the Roman numerals, so cumbrous were they. The number, for instance, which we represent by the figures 89 would require for its expression no less than *nine* figures, LXXXVIIII. The boy was helped by using the fingers, the left hand being used to signify numbers below a hundred, and the right numbers above it. Sometimes his teacher would have a counting-board, on which units, tens, and hundreds would be represented by variously colored balls. The sums which he did were mostly of a practical kind. Here is the sample that Horace gives of an arithmetic lesson. "The Roman boys are taught to divide the penny by long calculations. 'If from five ounces be subtracted one, what is the re-

mainder?' At once you can answer, 'A third
of a penny.' 'Good, you will be able to take
care of your money. If an ounce be added
what does it make?' 'The half of a penny.'"

While he was acquiring this knowledge he
was also learning a language, the one language
besides his own which to a Roman was worth
knowing—Greek. Very possibly he had begun
to pick it up in the nursery, where a Greek
slave girl was to be found, just as the French
bonne or the German nursery-governess is
among our own wealthier families. He certainly began to acquire it when he reached the
age at which his regular education was com-
menced. Cato the Elder, though he made it a
practice to teach his own sons, had nevertheless a Greek slave who was capable of undertaking the work, and who actually did teach, to
the profit of his very frugal master, the sons
of other nobles. Æmilius, the conqueror of
Macedonia, who was a few years younger than
Cato, had as a tutor a Greek of some distinction. While preparing the procession of his
triumph he had sent to Athens for a scene-
painter, as we should call him, who might make

pictures of conquered towns wherewith to illus-
trate his victories. He added to the commiss-
sion a stipulation that the artist should also be
qualified to take the place of tutor. By good
fortune the Athenians happened to have in
stock, so to speak, exactly the man he wanted,
one Metrodorus. Cicero had a Greek teacher
in his own family, not for his son indeed, who
was not born till later, but for his own benefit.
This was one Diodotus, a Stoic philosopher.
Cicero had been his pupil in his boyhood, and
gave him a home till the day of his death, " I
learned many things from him, logic especially."
In old age he lost his sight. "Yet," says his
pupil, " he devoted himself to study even more
diligently than before ; he had books read to
him night and day. These were studies which
he could pursue without his eyes ; but he
also, and this seems almost incredible, taught
geometry without them, instructing his learners
whence and whither the line was to be drawn,
and of what kind it was to be." It is interesting to know that when the old man died he left
his benefactor about nine thousand pounds.

Of course only wealthy Romans could command for their sons the services of such teachers as Diodotus ; but any well-to-do-household contained a slave who had more or less acquaintance with Greek. In Cicero's time a century and more of conquests on the part of Rome over Greek and Greek-speaking communities had brought into Italian families a vast number of slaves who knew the Greek language, and something, often a good deal, of Greek literature. One of these would probably be set apart as the boy's attendant ; from him he would learn to speak and read a language, a knowledge of which was at least as common at Rome as is a knowledge of French among English gentlemen.

If the Roman boy of whom we are speaking belonged to a very wealthy and distinguished family, he would probably receive his education at home. Commonly he would go to school. There were schools, girls' schools as well as boys' schools, at Rome in the days of the wicked Appius Claudius. The schoolmaster appears among the Etruscans in the story of Camillus, when the traitor, who offers to hand over to the Roman general the sons of the chief citizen of Falerii, is at his command scourged back into the town by his scholars. We find him again in the same story in the Latin town of Tusculum, where it is mentioned as one of the signs of a time of profound peace (Camillus had hurriedly marched against the town on a false report of its having revolted), that the hum of scholars at their lessons was heard in the market-place. At Rome, as time went on, and the Forum became more and more busy and noisy, the schools were removed to more suitable localities. Their appliances for teaching were improved and increased. Possibly maps were added, certainly reading books. Homer was read, and, as we have seen, the old Latin play-writers, and, afterwards, Virgil. Horace threatens the book which willfully insists on going out into the world with this fate, that old age will find it in a far-off suburb teaching boys their letters. Some hundred years afterwards the prophecy was fulfilled. Juvenal tells us how the schoolboys stood each with a lamp in one hand and a well-thumbed Horace or sooty Virgil in the other. Quintilian, writing about the same time, goes into detail, as becomes an old schoolmaster. " It is an admirable practice that the boy's reading should begin with Homer and Virgil. The tragic writers also are useful ; and there is much benefit to be got from the lyric poets also. But here you must make a selection not of authors only, but a part of authors." It is curious to find him banishing altogether a book that is, or certainly was, more extensively used in our schools than any other classic, the Heroides of Ovid.

These, and such as these, then, are the books which our Roman boy would have to read. Composition would not be forgotten. " Let him take," says the author just quoted, " the fables of Æsop and tell them in simple language, never rising above the ordinary level. Then let him pass on to a style less plain ; then, again, to bolder paraphrases, sometimes shortening, sometimes amplifying the original, but always following his sense." He also suggests the writing of themes and characters. One example he gives is this, " Was Crates the philosopher right when, having met an ignorant boy, he administered a beating to his teacher?" Many subjects of these themes have been preserved. Hannibal was naturally one often chosen. His passage of the Alps, and the question whether he should have advanced on the city immediately after the battle of Cannæ, were frequently discussed. Cicero mentions a subject of the speculative kind. " It is forbidden to a stranger to mount the wall. A. mounts the wall, but only to help the citizens in repelling their enemies. Has A. broken the law ? "

To make these studies more interesting to the Roman boy, his schoolmaster called in the aid of emulation. " I feel sure," says Quintilian, " that the practice which I remember to have been employed by my own teachers was any thing but useless. They were accustomed to divide the boys into classes, and they set us to speak in the order of our powers ; every one taking his turn according to his proficiency. Our performances were duly estimated ; and prod gious were the struggles which we had for victory. To be the head of one's class was considered the most glorious thing conceivable. But the decision was not made once for all. The next month brought the vanquished an

opportunity of renewing the contest. He who
had been victorious in the first encounter was
not led by success to relax his efforts, and a
feeling of vexation impelled the vanquished to
do away with the disgrace of defeat. This
practice, I am sure, supplied a keener stimulus
to learning than did all the exhortations of our
teachers, the care of our tutors, and the wishes
of our parents." Nor did the schoolmaster
trust to emulation alone. The third choice of
the famous Winchester line, " Either learn, or
go : there is yet another choice—to be flogged,"
was liberally employed. Horace celebrates his
old schoolmaster as a " man of many blows,"
and another distinguished pupil of this teacher,
the Busby or Keate of antiquity, has specified
the weapons which he employed, the ferule
and the thong. The thong is the familiar
"tawse" of schools north of the Border. The
ferule was a name given both to the bamboo
and to the yellow cane, which grew plentifully
both in the islands of the Greek Archipelago
and in Southern Italy, as notably at Cannæ in
Apulia, where it gave a name to the scene of
the great battle. The *virga* was also used, a

rod commonly of birch, a tree the educational use of which had been already discovered. The walls of Pompeii indeed show that the practice of Eton is truly classical down to its details.

As to the advantage of the practice opinions were divided. One enthusiastic advocate goes so far as to say that the Greek word for a cane signifies by derivation, " the sharpener of the young" (*narthex, nearous thegein*), but the best authorities were against it. Seneca is indignant with the savage who will " butcher" a young learner because he hesitates at a word—a venial fault indeed, one would think, when we re-member what must have been the aspect of a Roman book, written as it was in capitals, almost without stops, and with little or no dis-tinction between the words. And Quintilian is equally decided, though he allows that flog-ging was an " institution."

As to holidays the practice of the Roman schools probably resembled that which prevails in the Scotch Universities, though with a less magnificent length of vacation. Every one had a holiday on the "days of Saturn " (a festival beginning on the seventeenth of De-

A Roman Boy.

cember), and the schoolboys had one of their
own on the "days of Minerva," which fell in
the latter half of March ; but the "long vacation" was in the summer. Horace speaks
of lads carrying their fees to school on the
fifteenth of the month for eight months in the
year (if this interpretation of a doubtful passage
is correct). Perhaps as this was a country
school the holidays were made longer than
usual, to let the scholars take their part in the
harvest, which as including the vintage would
not be over till somewhat late in the autumn.
We find Martial, however, imploring a schoolmaster to remember that the heat of July was
not favorable to learning, and suggesting that
he should abdicate his seat till the fifteenth of
October brought a season more convenient for
study. Rome indeed was probably deserted
in the later summer and autumn by the wealthier
class, who were doubtless disposed to agree in
the poet's remark, a remark to which the idlest
schoolboy will forgive its Latin for the sake of
its admirable sentiment :

" Æstate pueri si valent satis discunt."
" In summer boys learn enough, if they keep their health."

Something, perhaps, may be said of the teachers, into whose hands the boys of Rome were committed. We have a little book, of not more than twoscore pages in all, which gives us "lives of illustrious schoolmasters;" and from which we may glean a few facts. The first business of a schoolmaster was to teach grammar, and grammar Rome owed, as she owed most of her knowledge, to a Greek, a certain Crates, who coming as ambassador from one of the kings of Asia Minor, broke his leg while walking in the ill-paved streets of Rome, and occupied his leisure by giving lectures at his house. Most of the early teachers were Greeks. Catulus bought a Greek slave for somewhat more than fifteen hundred pounds, and giving him his freedom set him up as a schoolmaster; another of the same nation received a salary of between three and four hundred pounds, his patron taking and probably making a considerable profit out of the pupils' fees. Orbilius, the man of blows, was probably of Greek descent. He had been first a beadle, then a trumpeter, then a trooper in his youth, and came to Rome in the year in which Cicero was consul. He seems

to have been as severe on the parents of his
pupils as he was in another way on the lads
themselves, for he wrote a book in which he
exposed their meanness and ingratitude. His
troubles, however, did not prevent him living to
the great age of one hundred and three. The
author of the little book about schoolmasters
had seen his statue in his native town. It was
a marble figure, in a sitting posture, with two
writing desks beside it. The favorite authors
of Orbilius, who was of the old-fashioned school,
were, as has been said, the early dramatists.
Cæcilius, a younger man, to whom Atticus the
friend and correspondent of Cicero gave his
freedom, lectured on Virgil, with whom, as he
was intimate with one of Virgil's associates,
he probably had some acquaintance. A
certain Flaccus had the credit of having first
invented prizes. He used to pit lads of equal
age against each other, supplying not only
a subject on which to write, but a prize for
the victor. This was commonly some handsome or rare old book. Augustus made him
tutor to his grandsons, giving him a salary of
eight hundred pounds per annum. Twenty

years later, a fashionable schoolmaster is said
to have made between three and four thousands.

These schoolmasters were also sometimes
teachers of eloquence, lecturing to men.   One
Gnipho, for instance, is mentioned among them,
as having held his classes in the house of Julius
Cæsar (Cæsar was left an orphan at fifteen) ;
and afterwards, when his distinguished pupil
was grown up, in his own.   But Cicero, when
he was prætor, and at the very height of his
fame, is said to have attended his lectures.
This was the year in which he delivered the
very finest of his non-political speeches, his
defence of Cluentius.   He must have been a
very clever teacher from whom so great an
orator hoped to learn something.

These teachers of eloquence were what we
may call the " Professors " of Rome.   A lad
had commonly "finished his education" when
he put on the "man's gown ;" but if he thought
of political life, of becoming a statesman, and
taking office in the commonwealth, he had
much yet to learn.   He had to make himself
a lawyer and an orator.   Law he learned by
attaching himself, by becoming the pupil, as

we should say, of some great man that was
famed for his knowledge. Cicero relates to us
his own experience: " My father introduced
me to the Augur Scævola ; and the result was
that, as far as possible and permissible, I never
left the old man's side. Thus I committed to
memory many a learned argument of his, many
a terse and clever maxim, while I sought to
add to my own knowledge from his stores of
special learning. When the Augur died I
betook myself to the Pontiff of the same name
and family." Elsewhere we have a picture of
this second Scævola and his pupils. " Though
he did not undertake to give instruction to any
one, yet he practically taught those who were
anxious to listen to him by allowing them to
hear his answers to those who consulted him."
These consultations took place either in the
Forum or at his own house. In the Forum
the great lawyer indicated that clients were at
liberty to approach by walking across the open
space from corner to corner. The train of
young Romans would then follow his steps,
just as the students follow the physician or
the surgeon through the wards of a hospital.

When he gave audience at home they would stand by his chair. It must be remembered that the great man took no payment either from client or from pupil.

But the young Roman had not only to learn law, he must also learn how to speak—learn, as far as such a thing can be learned, how to be eloquent. What we in this country call the career of the public man was there called the career of the orator. With us it is much a matter of chance whether a man can speak or not. We have had statesmen who wielded all the power that one man ever can wield in this country who had no sort of eloquence. We have had others who had this gift in the highest degree, but never reached even one of the lower offices in the government. Sometimes a young politician will go to a professional teacher to get cured of some defect or trick of speech ; but that such teaching is part of the necessary training of a statesman is an idea quite strange to us. A Roman received it as a matter of course. Of course, like other things at Rome, it made its way but slowly. Just before the middle of the second century B.C.

the Senate resolved : " Seeing that mention
has been made of certain philosophers and
rhetoricians, let Pomponius the prætor see to
it, as he shall hold it to be for the public good,
and for his own honor, that none such be
found at Rome." Early in the first century
the censors issued an edict forbidding certain
Latin rhetoricians to teach. One of these
censors was the great orator Crassus, greatest
of all the predecessors of Cicero. Cicero puts
into his mouth an apology for this proceeding :
" I was not actuated by any hostility to
learning or culture. These Latin rhetoricians
were mere ignorant pretenders, inefficient imi-
tators of their Greek rivals, from whom the
Roman youth were not likely to learn any thing
but impudence." In spite of the censors, however, and in spite of the fashionable belief in
Rome that what was Greek must be far better
than what was of native growth, the Latin
teachers rose into favor. " I remember," says
Cicero, "when we were boys, one Lucius
Plotinus, who was the first to teach eloquence
in Latin ; how, when the studious youth of the
capital crowded to hear him it vexed me much,

that I was not permitted to attend him. I was checked, however, by the opinion of learned men, who held that in this matter the abilities of the young were more profitably nourished by exercises in Greek." We are reminded of our own Doctor Johnson, who declared that he would not disgrace the walls of Westminster Abbey by an epitaph in English.

The chief part of the instruction which these teachers gave was to propose imaginary cases involving some legal difficulty for their pupils to discuss. One or two of these cases may be given.

One day in summer a party of young men from Rome made an excursion to Ostia, and coming down to the seashore found there some fishermen who were about to draw in a net. With these they made a bargain that they should have the draught for a certain sum. The money was paid. When the net was drawn up no fish were found in it, but a hamper sewn with thread of gold. The buyers allege this to be theirs as the draught of the net. The fishermen claim it as not being fish. To whom did it belong ?

Certain slave-dealers, landing a cargo of slaves at Brundisium, and having with them a very beautiful boy of great value, fearing' lest the custom-house officers should lay hands upon him, put upon him the *bulla* and the purple-edged robe that free-born lads were wont to wear. The deceit was not discovered. But when they came to Rome, and the matter was talked of, it was maintained that the boy was really free, seeing that it was his master who of his own free will had given him the token of freedom.

I shall conclude this chapter with a very pretty picture, which a Roman poet draws of the life which he led with his teacher in the days when he was first entering upon manhood. "When first my timid steps lost the guardianship of the purple stripe, and the *bulla* of the boy was hung up .for offering to the quaint household gods ; when flattering comrades came about me, and I might cast my eyes without rebuke over the whole busy street under the shelter of the yet unsullied gown ; in the days when the path is doubtful, and the wanderer knowing naught of life comes with

bewildered soul to the many-branching roads—
then I made myself your adopted child. You
took at once into the bosom of another
Socrates my tender years; your rule, applied
with skillful disguise, straightens each perverse
habit; nature is molded by reason, and struggles to be subdued, and assumes under your
hands its plastic lineaments. Ay, well I mind
how I would wear away long summer suns
with you, and pluck with you the bloom of
night's first hours. One work we had, one
certain time for rest, and at one modest table
unbent from sterner thoughts."

It accords with this charming picture to be
told that the pupil, dying in youth, left his
property to his old tutor, and that the latter
handed it over to the kinsfolk of the deceased,
keeping for himself the books only.

CHAPTER II.

A ROMAN UNDERGRADUATE.

In the last chapter we had no particular
"Roman Boy" in view; but our "Roman
Undergraduate" will be a real person, Cicero's
son. It will be interesting to trace the notices
which we find of him in his father's letters and
books. "You will be glad to hear," he writes
in one of his earliest letters to Atticus, "that
a little son has been born to me, and that Terentia is doing well." From time to time we
hear of him, and always spoken of in terms of
the tenderest affection. He is his "honey-
sweet Cicero," his "little philosopher." When
the father is in exile the son's name is put on
the address of his letters along with those of
his mother and sister. His prospects are the
subject of most anxious thought. Terentia,
who had a considerable fortune of her own,

proposes to sell an estate. "Pray think," he writes, "what will happen to us. If the same ill fortune shall continue to pursue us, what will happen to our unhappy boy? I cannot write any more. My tears fairly overpower me; I should be sorry to make you as sad as myself. I will say so much. If my friends do their duty by me, I shall not want for money; if they do not, your means will not save me. I do implore you, by all our troubles, do not ruin the poor lad. Indeed he is ruined enough already. If he has only something to keep him from want, then modest merit and moderate good fortune will give him all he wants."

Appointed to the government of Cilicia, Cicero takes his son with him into the province. When he starts on his campaign against the mountain tribes, the boy and his cousin, young Quintus, are sent to the court of Deiotarus, one of the native princes of Galatia. "The young Ciceros," he writes to Atticus, "are with Deiotarus. If need be, they will be taken to Rhodes." Atticus, it may be mentioned, was uncle to Quintus, and might be anxious about

him. The need was probably the case of the
old prince himself marching to Cicero's help.
This he had promised to do, but the campaign
was finished without him. This was in the
year 51 B.C., and Marcus was nearly fourteen
years old, his cousin being his senior by about
two years. "They are very fond of each other,"
writes Cicero; "they learn, they amuse themselves together, but one wants the rein, the
other the spur." (Doubtless the latter is the
writer's son.) "I am very fond of Dionysius
their teacher: the lads say that he is apt to get
furiously angry. But a more learned and more
blameless man there does not live." A year or
so afterwards he seems to have thought less
favorably of him. "I let him go reluctantly
when I thought of him as the tutor of the two
lads, but quite willingly as an ungrateful fellow."
In B.C. 49, when the lad was about half
through his sixteenth year, Cicero "gave him
his *toga*." To take the *toga*, that is to exchange
the gown of the boy with its stripe of purple
for the plain white gown of the citizen, marked
the beginning of independence (though indeed a
Roman's son was even in mature manhood under

his father's control). The ceremony took place at Arpinum, much to the delight of the inhabitants, who felt of course the greatest pride and interest in their famous fellow-townsman. But it was a sad time. "There and everywhere as I journeyed I saw sorrow and dismay. The prospect of this vast trouble is sad indeed." The "vast trouble" was the civil war between Cæsar and Pompey. This indeed had already broken out. While Cicero was entertaining his kinsfolk and friends at Arpinum, Pompey was preparing to fly from Italy. The war was probably not an unmixed evil to a lad who was just beginning to think himself a man. He hastened across the Adriatic to join his father's friend, and was appointed to the command of a squadron of auxiliary cavalry. His maneuvers were probably assisted by some veteran subordinate; but his seat on horseback, his skill with the javelin, and his general soldierly qualities were highly praised both by his chief and by his comrades. After the defeat at Pharsalia he waited with his father at Brundisium till a kind letter from Cæsar assured him of pardon. In B.C. 46 he was made ædile at Arpinum, his cousin being appointed at the same time. The next year he would have gladly resumed his military career. Fighting was going on in Spain, where the sons of Pompey were holding out against the forces of Cæsar; and the young Cicero, who was probably not very particular on which side he drew his sword, was ready to take service against the son of his old general. Neither the cause nor the career pleased the father, and the son's wish was overruled, just as an English lad has sometimes to give up the unremunerative profession of arms, when there is a living in the family, or an opening in a bank, or a promising connection with a firm of solicitors. It was settled that he should take up his residence at Athens, which was then the university of Rome, not indeed exactly in the sense in which Oxford and Cambridge are the universities of England, but still a place of liberal culture, where the sons of wealthy Roman families were accustomed to complete their education. Four-and-twenty years before the father had paid a long visit to the city, partly for study's sake. " In those days," he writes, " I was emaciated and feeble to a degree ; my neck was long and thin ; a habit of body and a figure that are thought to indicate much danger to life, if aggravated by a laborious profession and constant straining of the voice. My friends thought the more of this, because in those days I was accustomed to deliver all my speeches without any relaxation of effort, without any variety, at the very top of my voice, and with most abundant gesticulation. At first, when friends and physicians advised me to abandon advocacy for a while, I felt that I would sooner run any risk than relinquish the hope of oratorical distinction. Afterwards I reflected that by learning to moderate and regulate my voice, and changing my style of speaking, I might both avert the danger that threatened my health and also acquire a more self-controlled manner. It was a resolve to break through the habits I had formed that induced me to travel to the East. I had practiced for two years, and my name had become well known when I left Rome. Coming to Athens I spent six months with Antiochus, the most distinguished and learned philosopher of the Old Academy, than whom there was no wiser or more famous teacher. At the same time I practiced myself diligently under the care of Demetrius Syrus, an old and not undistinguished master of eloquence." To Athens, then, Cicero always looked back with affection. He hears, for instance, that Appius is going to build a portico at Eleusis. " Will you think me a fool," he writes to Atticus, "if I do the same at the Academy ? ' I think so,' you will say. But I love Athens, the very place, much ; and I shall be glad to have some memorial of me there."

The new undergraduate, as we should call him, was to have a liberal allowance. " He shall have as much as Publilius, as much as Lentulus the Flamen, allow their sons." It would be interesting to know the amount, but unhappily this cannot be recovered. All that we know is that the richest young men in Rome were not to have more. " I will guarantee," writes this liberal father, " that none of the three young men [whom he names] who, I hear, will be at Athens at the same time shall live at more expense than he will be able to do on those rents." These "rents" were the incomings from certain properties at Rome. "Only," he adds, "I do not think he will want a horse."

We know something of the university buildings, so to speak, which the young Cicero found at Athens. "To seek for truth among the groves of Academus" is the phrase by which a more famous contemporary, the poet Horace, describes his studies at Athens. He probably uses it generally to express philosophical pursuits; taken strictly it would mean that he attached himself to the sage whose pride it was to be the successor of Plato. Academus was a local hero, connected with the legend of Theseus and Helen. Near his grove, or sacred inclosure, which adjoined the road to Eleusis, Plato had bought a garden. It was but a small spot, purchased for a sum which may be represented by about three or four hundred pounds of our money, but it had been enlarged by the liberality of successive benefactors. This then was one famous lecture-room. Another was the Lyceum. Here Aristotle had taught, and after Aristotle, Theophrastus, and after him, a long succession of thinkers of the same school. A third institution of the same kind was the garden in which Epicurus had assembled his disciples, and which he bequeathed to trustees for their benefit and the benefit of their successors for all time.

To a Roman of the nobler sort these gardens and buildings must have been as holy places. It was with these rather than with the temples of gods that he connected what there was of goodness and purity in his life. To worship Jupiter or Romulus did not make him a better man, though it might be his necessary duty as a citizen ; his real religion, as we understand it, was his reverence for Plato or Zeno. Athens to him was not only what Athens, but what the Holy Land is to us. Cicero describes something of this feeling in the following passage : " We had been listening to Antiochus (a teacher of the Academics) in the school called the Ptolemæus, where he was wont to lecture. Marcus Piso was with me, and my brother Quintus, and Atticus, and Lucius Cicero, by relationship a cousin, in affection a brother. We agreed among ourselves to finish our afternoon walk in the Academy, chiefly because that place was sure not to be crowded at that hour.   At the proper time we met at Piso's house ; thence, occupied with varied talk, we traversed the six furlongs that lie between the Double Gate and the Academy ; and entering the walls which can give such good reason for their fame, found there the solitude which we sought.   'Is it,' said Piso, 'by some natural instinct or through some delusion that when we see the very spots where famous men have lived we are far more touched than when we hear of the things that they have done, or read something that they have written ?   It is thus that I am affected at this moment.   I think of Plato, who was, we are told, the first who lectured in this place ; his little garden which lies there close at hand seems not only to remind me of him, but actually to bring him up before my eyes.   Here spake Speusippus, here Xenocrates, here his disciple Polemo—to Polemo indeed belonged this seat which we have before us.'" This was the Polemo who had been converted, as we should say, when, bursting in after a night of revel upon a lecture in which Xenocrates was discoursing of temperance, he listened to such purpose that from that moment he became a changed man. Then Atticus describes how he found the same charms of association in the garden which had belonged to his own master, Epicurus ; while Quintus Cicero supplies what we should call the classical element by speaking of Sophocles and the grove of Colonus, still musical, it seems, with the same song of the nightingale which had charmed the ear of the poet more than three centuries before.

One or other, perhaps more than one, of these famous places the young Cicero frequented. He probably witnessed, he possibly took part (for strangers were admitted to membership) in, the celebrations with which the college of Athenian youths (Ephebi) commemorated the glories of their city, the procession to the tombs of those who died at Marathon, and the boat-races in the Bay of Salamis. That he gave his father some trouble is only too certain. His private tutor in rhetoric, as we should call him, was a certain Gorgias, a man of ability, and a writer of some note, but a worthless and profligate fellow. Cicero peremptorily ordered his son to dismiss him ; and the young man seems to have obeyed and reformed. We may hope at least that the repentance which he expresses for his misdoings in a letter to Tiro, his father's freed-man, was genuine. This is his picture of his life in the days of repentance and soberness: " I am on terms of the closest intimacy with Cratippus, living with him more as a son than as a pupil. Not only do I hear his lectures with delight, but I am greatly taken with the geniality which is peculiar to the man. I spend whole days with him, and often no small part of the night; for I beg him to dine with me as often as he can. This has become so habitual with him that he often looks in upon us at dinner when we are not expecting him; he lays aside the sternness of the philosopher and jokes with us in the pleasantest fashion. As for Bruttius, he never leaves me; frugal and strict as is his life, he is yet a most delightful companion. For we do not entirely banish mirth from our daily studies in philology. I have hired a lodging for him close by; and do my best to help his poverty out of my own narrow means. I have begun to practice Greek declamation with Cassius, and wish to have a Latin course

with Bruttius.   My friends and daily companions are the pupils whom Cratippus brought
with him from Mitylene, well-read men, of whom
he highly approves.   I also see much of Epi-
crates, who is the first man at Athens."   After
some pleasant words to Tiro, who had bought a
farm, and whom he expects to find turned into
a farmer, bringing stores, holding consultations
with his bailiff, and putting by fruit-seeds in his
pocket from dessert, he says, " I should be glad
if you would send me as quickly as possible
a copyist, a Greek by preference.   I have to
spend much pains on writing out my notes."

A short time before one of Cicero's friends
had sent a satisfactory report of the young
man's behavior to his father.   " I found your
son devoted to the most laudable studies and
enjoying an excellent reputation for steadiness.
Don't fancy, my dear Cicero, that I say this
to please you ; there is not in Athens a more
lovable young man than your son, nor one
more devoted to those high pursuits in which
you would have him interested."

Among the contemporaries of the young
Cicero was, as has been said, the poet Horace.

His had been a more studious boyhood. He had not been taken away from his books to serve as a cavalry officer under Pompey. In him accordingly we see the regular course of the studies of a Roman lad. " It was my lot," he says, " to be bred up at Rome, and to be taught how much the wrath of Achilles harmed the Greeks. In other words, he had read his Homer, just as an English boy reads him at Eton or Harrow. " Kind Athens," he goes on, " added a little more learning, to the end that I might be able to distinguish right from wrong, and to seek for truth amongst the groves of Academus." And just in the same way the English youth goes on to read philosophy at Oxford.

The studies of the two young men were interrupted by the same cause, the civil war which followed the death of Cæsar. They took service with Brutus, both having the same rank, that of military tribune, a command answering more or less nearly to that of colonel in our own army. It was, however, mainly an ornamental rank, being bestowed sometimes by favor of the general in command, sometimes

by a popular vote. The young Cicero indeed
had already served, and he now distinguished
himself greatly, winning some considerable successes in the command of the cavalry which
Brutus afterwards gave him. When the hopes
of the party were crushed at Phillippi, he
joined the younger Pompey in Sicily; but
took an opportunity of an amnesty which was
offered four years afterwards to return to
Rome. Here he must have found his old
fellow-student, who had also reconciled himself
to the victorious party. He was made one of
the college of augurs, and also a commissioner
of the mint, and in B.C. 30 he had the honour of
sharing the consulship with Augustus himself.
It was to him that the dispatch announcing the
final defeat and death of Antony was delivered;
and it fell to him to execute the decree which
ordered the destruction of all the statues of the
fallen chief. " Then," says Plutarch, "by the
ordering of heaven the punishment of Antony
was inflicted at last by the house of Cicero."
His time of office ended, he went as Governor
to Asia, or, according to some accounts, to
Syria; and thus disappears from our view.

Pliny the Elder tells us that he was a drunkard, sarcastically observing that he sought to avenge himself on Antony by robbing him of the reputation which he had before enjoyed of being the hardest drinker of the time. As the story which he tells of the younger Cicero being able to swallow twelve pints of wine at a draught is clearly incredible, perhaps we may disbelieve the whole, and with it the other anecdote, that he threw a cup at the head of Marcus Agrippa, son-in-law to the Emperor, and after him the greatest man in Rome.

CHAPTER III.

In November 82 B.C., Cornelius Sulla became
absolute master of Rome. It is not part of my
purpose to give a history of this man. He was
a great soldier who had won victories in Africa
and Asia over the enemies of Rome, and in
Italy itself over the " allies," as they were
called, that is the Italian nations, who at
various times had made treaties with Rome,
and who in the early part of the first century
B.C. rebelled against her, thinking that they
were robbed of the rights and privileges which
belonged to them. And he was the leader of
the party of the nobles, just as Marius was the
leader of the party of the people. Once before
he had made himself supreme in the capital ;
and then he had used his power with moderation. But he was called away to carry on
the war in Asia against Mithridates, the great

King of Pontus ; and his enemies had got the upper hand, and had used the opportunity most cruelly.   A terrible list of victims, called the " proscription," because it was posted up in the forum, was prepared.   Fifty senators and a thousand knights (peers and gentlemen we should call them) were put to death, almost all of them without any kind of trial.   Sulla himself was outlawed.   But he had an army which he had led to victory and had enriched with prize-money, and which was entirely devoted to him ; and he was not inclined to let his enemies triumph.   He hastened back to Italy, and landed in the spring of 83.   In the November of the following year, just outside the walls of Rome, was fought the final battle of the war. The opposing army was absolutely destroyed and Sulla had every thing at his mercy.   He waited for a few days outside the city till the Senate had passed a decree giving him absolute power to change the laws, to fill the offices of State, and to deal with the lives and properties of citizens as it might please him.   This done, he entered Rome.   Then came another proscription.   The chief of his enemies, Marius, was gone. He had died, tormented it was said by remorse, seventeen days after he had reached the crowning glory, promised him in his youth by an oracle, and had been made consul for the seventh time. The conqueror had to content himself with the same vengeance that Charles II. in our own country exacted from the remains of Cromwell. The ashes of Marius were taken out of his tomb on the Flaminian Way, the great North Road of Rome, and were thrown into the Anio. But many of his friends and partisans survived, and these were slaughtered without mercy. Eighty names were put on the fatal list on the first day, two hundred and twenty on the second, and as many more on the third. With the deaths of many of these victims politics had nothing to do. Sulla allowed his friends and favorites to put into the list the names of men against whom they happened to bear a grudge, or whose property they coveted. No one knew who might be the next to fall. Even Sulla's own partisans were alarmed. A young senator, Caius Metellus, one of a family which was strongly attached to Sulla and with which he was connected by

marriage, had the courage to ask him in public
when there would be an end to this terrible state
of things. "We do not beg you," he said, "to
remit the punishment of those whom you have
made up your mind to remove; we do beg you
to do away with the anxiety of those whom you
have resolved to spare." "I am not yet certain,"
answered Sulla, "whom I shall spare." "Then
at least," said Metellus, "you can tell us whom
you mean to punish." "That I will do," replied
the tyrant. It was indeed a terrible time that
followed. Plutarch thus describes it: "He
denounced against any who might shelter or
save the life of a proscribed person the punishment of death for his humanity. He made no
exemption for mother, or son, or parent. The
murderers received a payment of two talents
(about £470) for each victim; it was paid to a
slave who killed his master, to a son who killed
his father. The most monstrous thing of all, it
was thought, was that the sons and grandsons
of the proscribed were declared to be legally
infamous and that their property was confiscated. Nor was it only in Rome but in all the
cities of Italy that the proscription was carried

out. There was not a single temple, not a house but was polluted with blood. Husbands were slaughtered in the arms of their wives, and sons in the arms of their mothers. And the number of those who fell victims to anger and hatred was but small in comparison with the number who were put out of the way for the sake of their property. The murderers might well have said : ' His fine mansion has been the death of this man ; or his gardens, or his baths.' Quintus Aurelius, a peaceable citizen, who had had only this share in the late civil troubles, that he had felt for the misfortunes of others, coming into the forum, read the list of the proscribed and found in it his own name. ' Unfortunate that I am,' he said, ' it is my farm at Alba that has been my ruin ; ' and he had not gone many steps before he was cut down by a man that was following him. Lucius Catiline's conduct was especially wicked. He had murdered his own brother. This was before the proscription began. He went to Sulla and begged that the name might be put in the list as if the man were still alive ; and it was so put. His gratitude to Sulla was shown by his killing one Marius,

who belonged to the opposite faction, and bringing his head to Sulla as he sat in the forum.
(This Marius was a kinsman of the great democratic leader, and was one of the most popular
men in Rome.) This done, he washed his hands
in the holy water-basin of the temple of Apollo."

Forty senators and sixteen hundred knights,
and more than as many men of obscure station,
are said to have perished. At last, on the first
of June, 81, the list was closed. Still the reign
of terror was not yet at an end, as the strange
story which I shall now relate will amply prove.
To look into the details of a particular case
makes us better able to imagine what it really
was to live at Rome in the days of the Dictator
than to read many pages of general description.
The story is all the more impressive because
the events happened after order had been
restored and things were supposed to be proceeding in their regular course.

The proscription came to an end, as has
been said, in the early summer of 81. In the
autumn of the same year a certain Sextus
Roscius was murdered in the streets of Rome
as he was returning home from dinner.

A SENATOR.

Roscius was a native of Ameria, a little town of Etruria, between fifty and sixty miles north of Rome. He was a wealthy man, possessed, it would seem, of some taste and culture, and an intimate friend of some of the noblest families at Rome. In politics he belonged to the party of Sulla, to which indeed in its less prosperous days he had rendered good service. Since its restoration to power he had lived much at Rome, evidently considering himself, as indeed he had the right to do, to be perfectly safe from any danger of proscription. But he was wealthy, and he had among his own kins-folk enemies who desired and who would profit by his death. One of these, a certain Titus Roscius, surnamed Magnus, was at the time of the murder residing at Rome; the other, who was known as Capito, was at home at Ameria. The murder was committed about seven o'clock in the evening. A messenger immediately left Rome with the news, and made such haste to Ameria that he reached the place before dawn the next day. Strangely enough he went to the house not of the murdered man's son, who was living at Ameria in charge of his farms, but of the hostile kinsman Capito. Three days afterwards Capito and Magnus made their way to the camp of Sulla (he was besieging Volaterræ, another Etrurian town). They had an interview with one Chrysogonus, a Greek freedman of the Dictator, and explained to him how rich a prey they could secure if he would only help them. The deceased, it seems, had left a large sum of money and thirteen valuable farms, nearly all of them running down to the Tiber. And the son, the lawful heir, could easily be got out of the way. Roscius was a well-known and a popular man, yet no outcry had followed his disappearance. With the son, a simple farmer, ignorant of affairs, and wholly unknown to Rome, it would be easy to deal. Ultimately the three entered into alliance. The proscription was to be revived, so to speak, to take in this particular case, and the name of Roscius was included in the list of the condemned. All his wealth was treated as the property of the proscribed, and was sold by auction. It was purchased by Chrysogonus. The real value was between fifty and sixty thousand pounds.

The price paid was something less than eighteen pounds. Three of the finest farms were at once handed over to Capito as his share of the spoil. Magnus acted as the agent of Chrysogonus for the remainder. He took possession of the house in which Roscius the younger was living, laid his hands on all its contents, among which was a considerable sum of money, and drove out the unfortunate young man in an absolutely penniless condition.

These proceedings excited great indignation at Ameria. The local senate passed a resolution to the effect that the committee of ten should proceed to Sulla's camp and put him in possession of the facts, with the object of removing the name of the father from the list of the proscribed, and reinstating the son in his inheritance. The ten proceeded accordingly to the camp, but Chrysogonus cajoled and overreached them. It was represented to them by persons of high position that there was no need to trouble Sulla with the affair. The name should be removed from the list; the property should be restored. Capito, who was one of the ten, added his personal assurance to the same effect, and the deputation, satisfied that their object had been attained, returned to Ameria. There was of course no intention of fulfilling the promises thus made. The first idea of the trio was to deal with the son as they had dealt with the father. Some hint of this purpose was conveyed to him, and he fled to Rome, where he was hospitably entertained by Cæcilia, a wealthy lady of the family of Metellus, and therefore related to Sulla's wife, who indeed bore the same name. As he was now safe from violence, it was resolved to take the audacious step of accusing him of the murder of his father. Outrageous as it seems, the plan held out some promise of success. The accused was a man of singularly reserved character, rough and boorish in manner, and with no thoughts beyond the rustic occupations to which his life was devoted. His father, on the other hand, had been a man of genial temper, who spent much of his time among the polished circles of the Capitol. If there was no positive estrangement between them, there was a great discrepancy of tastes, and probably very little intercourse. This it would be easy to exaggerate into something like a plausible charge, especially under the circumstances of the case. It was beyond doubt that many murders closely resembling the murder of Roscius had been committed during the past year, committed some of them by sons. This was the first time that an alleged culprit was brought to trial, and it was probable that the jury would be inclined to severity. In any case, and whatever the evidence, it was hoped that the verdict would not be such as to imply the guilt of a favorite of Sulla. He was the person who would profit most by the condemnation of the accused, and it was hoped that he would take the necessary means to secure it.

The friends of the father were satisfied of the innocence of the son, and they exerted themselves to secure for him an efficient defense. Sulla was so much dreaded that none of the more conspicuous orators of the time were willing to undertake the task. Cicero, however, had the courage which they wanted ; and his speech, probably little altered from the form in which he delivered it, remains. It was a horrible crime of which his client was accused, and the punishment the most awful known to the Roman law. The face of the guilty man was covered with a wolf's skin, as being one who was not worthy to see the light; shoes of wood were put upon his feet that they might not touch the earth. He was then thrust into a sack of leather, and with him four animals which were supposed to symbolize all that was most hideous and depraved—the dog, a common object of contempt; the cock, proverbial for its want of all filial affection; the poisonous viper; and the ape, which was the base imitation of man. In this strange company he was thrown into the nearest river or sea.

Cicero begins by explaining why he had undertaken a case which his elders and betters had declined. It was not because he was bolder, but because he was more insignificant than they, and could speak with impunity when they could not choose but be silent. He then gives the facts in detail, the murder of Roscius, the seizure of his property, the fruitless depu-tation to Sulla, the flight of the son to Rome, and the audacious resolve of his enemies to indict him for parricide. They had murdered

his father, they had robbed him of his patrimony, and now they accused him—of what
crime? Surely of nothing else than the crime
of having escaped their attack. The thing
reminded him of the story of Fimbria and
Scævola. Fimbria, an absolute madman, as
was allowed by all who were not mad themselves, got some ruffian to stab Scævola at
the funeral of Marius. He was stabbed but
not killed. When Fimbria found that he was
likely to live, he indicted him. For what do
you indict a man so blameless? asked some
one. For what? for not allowing himself to
be stabbed to the heart. This is exactly why
the confederates have indicted Roscius. His
crime has been of escaping from their hands,
" Roscius killed his father," you say. " A young
man, I suppose, led away by worthless companions." Not so; he is more than forty years
of age. " Extravagance and debt drove him to
it." No; you say yourself that he never goes
to an entertainment, and he certainly owes
nothing. " Well," you say, " his father disliked
him." Why did he dislike him? "That,"
you reply, " I cannot say; but he certainly

kept one son with him, and left this Roscius to look after his farms." Surely this is a strange punishment, to give him the charge of so fine an estate. "But," you repeat, "he kept his other with him." "Now listen to me," cries Cicero, turning with savage sarcasm to the prosecutor, "Providence never allowed you to know who your father was. Still you have read books. Do you remember in Cæcilius' play how the father had two sons, and kept one with him and left the other in the country? and do you remember that the one who lived with him was not really his son, the other was true-born, and yet it was the true-born who lived in the country? And is it such a disgrace to live in the country? It is well that you did not live in old times when they took a Dictator from the plow; when the men who made Rome what it is cultivated their own land, but did not covet the land of others. 'Ah! but,' you say, 'the father intended to disinherit him.' Why? 'I cannot say.' Did he disinherit him? 'No, he did not.' Who stopped him? 'Well, he was thinking of it.' To whom did he say so? 'To no one.'

Surely," cries Cicero, "this is to abuse the laws and justice and your dignity in the basest and most wanton way, to make charges which he not only cannot but does not even attempt to establish."

Shortly after comes a lively description of the prosecutor's demeanor. "It was really worth while, if you observed, gentlemen, the man's utter indifference as he was conducting his case. I take it that when he saw who was sitting on these benches, he asked whether such an one or such an one was engaged for the defense. Of me he never thought, for I had never spoken before in a criminal case. When he found that none of the usual speakers were concerned in it, he became so careless that when the humor took him, he sat down, then walked about, sometimes called a servant, to give him orders, I suppose, for dinner, and certainly treated this court in which you are sitting as if it were an absolute solitude. At last he brought his speech to an end. I rose to reply. He could be seen to breathe again that it was I and no one else. I noticed, gentlemen, that he continued to laugh and be inattentive till I mentioned Chrysogonus. As soon as I got to him my friend roused himself and was evidently astonished. I saw what had touched him, and repeated the name a second time, and a third. From that time men have never ceased to run briskly backwards and forwards, to tell Chrysogonus, I suppose, that there was some one in the country who ventured to oppose his pleasure, that the case was being pleaded otherwise than as he imagined it would be ; that the sham sale of goods was being exposed, the confederacy grievously handled, his popularity and power disregarded, that the people were giving their whole attention to the cause, and that the common opinion was that the transaction generally was disgraceful.

" Then," continued the speaker, " this charge of parricide, so monstrous is the crime, must have the very strongest evidence to support it. There was a case at Tarracina of a man being found murdered in the chamber where he was sleeping, his two sons, both young men, being in the same room. No one could be found, either slave or free man, who seemed likely to have done the deed ; and as the two sons, grown up as they were, declared that they knew nothing about it, they were indicted for parricide. What could be so suspicious ? Suspicious, do I say ? Nay, worse. That neither knew any thing about it ? That any one had ventured into that chamber at the very time when there were in it two young men who would certainly perceive and defeat the attempt ? Yet, because it was proved to the jury that the young men had been found fast asleep, with the door wide open, they were acquitted. It was thought incredible that men who had just committed so monstrous a crime could possibly sleep. Why, Solon, the wisest of all legislators, drawing up his code of laws, provided no punishment for this crime ; and when he was asked the reason replied that he believed that no one would ever commit it. To provide a punishment would be to suggest rather than prevent. Our own ancestors provided indeed a punishment, but it was of the strangest kind, showing how strange, how monstrous they thought the crime. And what evidence do you bring forward ? The man was not at Rome. That is proved. There-

fore he must have done it, if he did it at all, by
the hands of others. Who were these others?
Were they free men or slaves? If they were
free men where did they come from, where
live? How did he hire them? Where is the
proof? You haven't a shred of evidence, and
yet you accuse him of parricide. And if they
were slaves, where, again I ask, are they?
There *were* two slaves who saw the deed; but
they belonged to the confederate not to the
accused. Why do you not produce them?
Purely because they would prove your guilt.

"It is there indeed that we find the real truth
of the matter. It was the maxim of a famous
lawyer, Ask: *who profited by the deed?* I ask
it now. It was Magnus who profited. He was
poor before, and now he is rich. And then
he was in Rome at the time of the murder; and
he was familiar with assassins. Remember too
the strange speed with which he sent the news
to Ameria, and sent it, not to the son, as one
might expect, but to Capito his accomplice;
for that he was an accomplice is evident enough.
What else could he be when he so cheated the
deputation that went to Sulla at Volaterræ?"

Cicero then turned to Chrysogonus, and attacked him with a boldness which is surprising, when we remember how high he stood in the favor of the absolute master of Rome, " See how he comes down from his fine mansion on the Palatine. Yes, and he has for his own enjoyment a delightful retreat in the suburbs, and many an estate besides, and not one of them but is both handsome and conveniently near. His house is crowded with ware of Corinth and Delos, among them that famous self-acting cooking apparatus, which he lately bought at a price so high that the passers-by, when they heard the clerk call out the highest bid, supposed that it must be a farm which was being sold. And what quantities, think you, he has of embossed plate, and coverlets of purple, and pictures, and statues, and colored marbles ! Such quantities, I tell you, as scarce could be piled together in one mansion in a time of tumult and rapine from many wealthy establishments. And his household— why should I describe how many it numbers, and how varied are its accomplishments ? I do not speak of ordinary domestics, the cook, the baker, the litter-bearer. Why, for the mere enjoyment of his ears he has such a multitude of men that the whole neighborhood echoes again with the daily music of singers, and harp-players, and flute-players, and with the uproar of his nightly banquets. What daily expenses, what extravagance, as you well know, gentlemen, there must be in such a life as this ! how costly must be these banquets ! Creditable banquets, indecd, held in such a house—a house, do I say, and not a manufactory of wickedness, a place of entertainment for every kind of crime ? And as for the man himself—you see, gentlemen, how he bustles every where about the forum, with his hair fashionably arranged and dripping with perfumes ; what a crowd of citizens, yes, of citizens, follow him ; you see how he looks down upon every one, thinks no one can be compared to himself, fancies himself the one rich and powerful man in Rome ? "

The jury seems to have caught the contagion of courage from the advocate. They acquitted the accused. It is not known whether he ever recovered his property. But as Sulla retired from power in the following year, and died the year after, we may hope that the favorites and the villains whom he had sheltered were compelled to disgorge some at least of their gains.

CHAPTER IV.

A ROMAN MAGISTRATE.

Of all the base creatures who found a profit in the massacers and plunderings which Sulla commanded or permitted, not one was baser than Caius Verres. The crimes that he committed would be beyond our belief if it were not for the fact that he never denied them. He betrayed his friends, he perverted justice, he plundered a temple with as little scruple as he plundered a private house, he murdered a citizen as boldly as he murdered a foreigner; in fact, he was the most audacious, the most cruel, the most shameless of men. And yet he rose to high office at home and abroad, and had it not been for the courage, sagacity, and eloquence of one man, he might have risen to the very highest. What Roman citizens had sometimes, and Roman subjects, it is to be feared, very often to endure may be seen from the picture which we are enabled to draw of a *Roman magistrate*.

Roman politicians began public life as quæs- tors. (A quæstor was an official who managed money matters for higher magistrates. Every governor of a province had one or more quæstors under him. They were elected at Rome, and their posts were assigned to them by lot.) Verres was quæstor in Gaul and em- bezzled the public money ; he was quæstor in Cilicia with Dolabella, a like-minded governor, and diligently used his opportunity. This time it was not money only, but works of art, on which he laid his hands ; and in these the great cities, whether in Asia or in Europe, were still rich. The most audacious, perhaps, of these robberies was perpetrated in the island of Delos. Delos was known all over the world as the island of Apollo. The legend was that it was the birthplace of the god. None of his shrines was more frequented or more famous. Verres was indifferent to such considerations. He stripped the temple of its finest statues, and loaded a merchant ship which he had hired with the booty. But this time he was not lucky enough to secure it. The islanders, though they had discovered the theft, did not, indeed, venture to complain. They thought it was the doing of the governor, and a governor, though his proceedings might be impeached after his term of office, was not a person with whom it was safe to remonstrate. But a terrible storm suddenly burst upon the island. The governor's departure was delayed. To set sail in such weather was out of the question. The sea was indeed so high that the town became scarcely habitable. Then Verres' ship was wrecked, and the statues were found cast upon the shore. The governor ordered them to be replaced in the temple, and the storm subsided as suddenly as it had arisen.

On his return to Rome Dolabella was impeached for extortion. With characteristic baseness Verres gave evidence against him, evidence so convincing as to cause a verdict of guilty. But he thus secured his own gains, and these he used so profusely in the purchase of votes that two or three years afterwards he was elected prætor. The prætors performed various functions which were assigned to them by lot. Chance, or it may possibly have been contrivance, gave to Verres the most considerable of them all. He was made " Prætor of the City ; " that is, a judge before whom a certain class of very important causes were tried. Of course he showed himself scandalously unjust. One instance of his proceedings may suffice.

A certain Junius had made a contract for keeping the temple of Castor in repair. When Verres came into office he had died, leaving a son under age. There had been some neglect, due probably to the troubles of the times, in seeing that the contracts had been duly executed, and the Senate passed a resolution that Verres and one of his fellow-prætors should see to the matter. The temple of Castor came under review like the others, and Verres, knowing that the original contractor was dead, inquired who was the responsible person. When he heard of the son under age he recognized at once a golden opportunity. It was one of the maxims which he had laid down for his own guidance, and which he had even been wont to

give out for the benefit of his friends, that much
profit might be made out of the property of
wards.   It had been arranged that the guardian
of the young Junius should take the contract
into his own hands, and, as the temple was in
excellent repair, there was no difficulty in the
way. Verres summoned the guardian to appear
before him.   "Is there any thing," he asked,
"that your ward has not made good, and which
we ought to require of him ? " "No," said he,
"every thing is quite right ; all the statues and
offerings are there, and the fabric is in excellent
repair."   From the prætor's point of view this
was not satisfactory ; and he determined on a
personal visit.   Accordingly he went to the
temple, and inspected it.   The ceiling was excellent ; the whole building in the best repair.
"What is to be done ? " he asked of one of his
satellites.   "Well," said the man, "there is
nothing for you to meddle with here, except
possibly to require that the columns should be
restored to the perpendicular."   "Restored to
the perpendicular ? what do you mean ?" said
Verres, who knew nothing of architecture.   It
was explained to him that it very seldom hap-

pened that a column was absolutely true to the
perpendicular. "Very good," said Verres; "we
will have the columns made perpendicular."
Notice accordingly was sent to the lad's
guardians. Disturbed at the prospect of indef-
inite loss to their ward's property, they sought
an interview with Verres. One of the noble
family of Marcellus waited upon him, and
remonstrated against the iniquity of the proceeding. The remonstrance was in vain. The
prætor showed no signs of relenting. There
yet remained one way, a way only too well
known to all who had to deal with him, of
obtaining their object. Application must be
made to his mistress (a Greek freedwoman of
the name of Chelidon or "The Swallow"). If
she could be induced to take an interest in the
case something might yet be done. Degrading
as such a course must have been to men of rank
and honor, they resolved, in the interest of
their ward, to take it. They went to Chelidon's house. It was thronged with people who
were seeking favors from the prætor. Some
were begging for decisions in their favor; some
for fresh trials of their cases. "I want posses-

sion," cried one. " He must not take the property from me," said another. " Don't let him pronounce judgment against me," cried a third. " The property must be assigned to me," was the demand of a fourth. Some were counting out money ; others signing bonds. The deputation, after waiting awhile, were admitted to the presence. Their spokesman explained the case, begged for Chelidon's assistance, and promised a substantial consideration. The lady was very gracious. She would willingly do what she could, and would talk to the prætor about it. The deputation must come again the next day and hear how she had succeeded. They came again, but found that nothing could be done. Verres felt sure that a large sum of money was to be got out of the proceeding, and resolutely refused any compromise.

They next made an offer of about two thousand pounds. This again was rejected. Verres resolved that he would put up the contract to auction, and did his best that the guardians should have no notice of it. Here, however, he failed. They attended the auction and made a bid. Of course the lowest bidder ought to have been accepted, so long as he gave security for doing the work well. But Verres refused to accept it. He knocked down the contract to himself at a price of more than five thousand pounds, and this though there were persons willing to do it for less than a sixth of that sum. As a matter of fact very little was done. Four of the columns were pulled down and built up again with the same stones. Others were whitewashed ; some had the old cement taken out and fresh put in.[1] The highest estimate for all that could possibly be wanted was less than eight hundred pounds.

His year of office ended, Verres was sent as governor to Sicily. By rights he should have remained there twelve months only, but his successor was detained by the Servile war in Italy, and his stay was thus extended to nearly three years, three years into which he crowded an incredible number of cruelties and robberies. Sicily was perhaps the wealthiest of all the provinces. Its fertile wheat-fields yielded harvests which, now that agriculture had begun to decay in Italy, provided no small part of the daily bread of Rome. In its cities, founded

[1] " Pointed," I suppose.

most of them several centuries before by colonists from Greece, were accumulated the riches of many generations. On the whole it had been lightly treated by its Roman conquerors. Some of its states had early discerned which would be the winning side, and by making their peace in time had secured their privileges and possessions. Others had been allowed to surrender themselves on favorable terms. This wealth had now been increasing without serious disturbance for more than a hundred years. The houses of the richer class were full of the rich tapestries of the East, of gold and silver plate cunningly chased or embossed, of statues and pictures wrought by the hands of the most famous artists of Greece. The temples were adorned with costly offerings and with images that were known all over the civilized world. The Sicilians were probably prepared to pay something for the privilege of being governed by Rome. And indeed the privilege was not without its value. The days of freedom indeed were over ; but the turbulence, the incessant strife, the bitter struggles between neighbors and parties were also at an

end. Men were left to accumulate wealth and
to enjoy it without hindrance. Any moderate
demands they were willing enough to meet.
They did not complain, for instance, or at least
did not complain aloud, that they were compelled to supply their rulers with a fixed quantity
of corn at prices lower than could have been
obtained in the open market. And they would
probably have been ready to secure the good
will of a governor who fancied himself a connoisseur in art with handsome presents from
their museums and picture galleries. But the
exactions of Verres exceeded all bounds both of
custom and of endurance. The story of how he
dealt with the wheat-growers of the province is
too tedious and complicated to be told in this
place. Let it suffice to say that he enriched
himself and his greedy troop of followers at the
cost of absolute ruin both to the cultivators of
the soil and to the Roman capitalists who
farmed this part of the public revenue. As to
the way in which he laid his hands on the possessions of temples and of private citizens, his
doings were emphatically summed up by his
prosecutor when he came, as we shall afterwards

see, to be put upon his trial. " I affirm that in the whole of Sicily, wealthy and old-established province as it is, in all those towns, in all those wealthy homes, there was not a single piece of silver plate, a single article of Corinthian or Delian ware, a single jewel or pearl, a single article of gold or ivory, a single picture, whether on panel or on canvas, which he did not hunt up and examine, and, if it pleased his fancy, abstract. This is a great thing to say, you think. Well, mark how I say it. It is not for the sake of rhetorical exaggeration that I make this sweeping assertion, that I declare that this fellow did not leave a single article of the kind in the whole province. I speak not in the language of the professional accuser but in plain Latin. Nay, I will put it more clearly still : in no single private house, in no town ; in no place, profane or even sacred ; in the hands of no Sicilian, of no citizen of Rome, did he leave a single article, public or private property, of things profane or things religious, which came under his eyes or touched his fancy."

Some of the more remarkable of these acts of spoliation it may be worth while to relate.

A certain Heius, who was at once the wealthiest
and most popular citizen of Messana, had a
private chapel of great antiquity in his house,
and in it four statues of the very greatest value.
There was a Cupid by Praxiteles, a replica of a
famous work which attracted visitors to the un-
interesting little town of Thespiæ in Bœotia ; a
Hercules from the chisel of Myro ; and two
bronze figures, " Basket-bearers," as they were
called, because represented as carrying sacred
vessels in baskets on their heads. These were
the work of Polyclitus. The Cupid had been
brought to Rome to ornament the forum on
some great occasion, and had been carefully
restored to its place. The chapel and its contents was the great sight of the town. No one
passed through without inspecting it. It was
naturally, therefore, one of the first things that
Verres saw, Messana being on his route to the
capital of his province. He did not actually
take the statues, he bought them ; but the price
that he paid was so ridiculously low that purchase was only another name for robbery.
Something near sixty pounds was given for the
four. If we recall the prices that would be paid

now-a-days for a couple of statues by Michael Angelo and two of the masterpieces of Raphael and Correggio, we may imagine what a monstrous fiction this sale must have been, all the more monstrous because the owner was a wealthy man, who had no temptation to sell, and who was known to value his possessions not only as works of art but as adding dignity to his hereditary worship.

A wealthy inhabitant of Tyndaris invited the governor to dinner. He was a Roman citizen and imagined that he might venture on a display which a provincial might have considered to be dangerous. Among the plate on the table was a silver dish adorned with some very fine medallions. It struck the fancy of the guest, who promptly had it removed, and who considered himself to be a marvel of moderation when he sent it back with the medallions abstracted.

His secretary happened one day to receive a letter which bore a noteworthy impression on the composition of chalk which the Greeks used for sealing. It attracted the attention of Verres, who inquired from what place it had come. Hearing that it had been sent from Agrigentum, he communicated to his agents in that town his desire that the seal-ring should be at once secured for him. And this was done. The unlucky possessor, another Roman citizen, by the way, had his ring actually drawn from his finger.

A still more audacious proceeding was to rob, not this time a mere Sicilian provincial or a simple Roman citizen, but one of the tributary kings, the heir of the great house of Antiochus, which not many years before had matched itself with the power of Rome. Two of the young princes had visited Rome, intending to prosecute their claims to the throne of Egypt, which, they contended, had come to them through their mother. The times were not favorable to the suit, and they returned to their country, one of them, Antiochus, probably the elder, choosing to take Sicily on his way. He naturally visited Syracuse, where Verres was residing, and Verres at once recognized a golden opportunity. The first thing was to send the visitor a handsome supply of wine, olive-oil, and wheat. The next was to invite him to

dinner. The dining-room and table were richly
furnished, the silver plate being particularly
splendid. Antiochus was highly delighted with
the entertainment, and lost no time in returning the compliment. The dinner to which he
invited the governor was set out with a splendor to which Verres had nothing to compare.
There was silver plate in abundance, and there
were also cups of gold, these last adorned
with magnificent gems.

Conspicuous among the ornaments of the
table was a drinking vessel, all in one piece,
probably of amethyst, and with a handle of
gold. Verres expressed himself delighted with
what he saw. He handled every vessel and
was loud in its praises. The simple-minded
King, on the other hand, heard the compliment
with pride. Next day came a message. Would
the King lend some of the more beautiful cups
to his excellency? He wished to show them
to his own artists. A special request was made
for the amethyst cup. All was sent without a
suspicion of danger.

But the King had still in his possession
something that especially excited the Roman's

cupidity. This was a candelabrum of gold richly
adorned with jewels. It had been intended for
an offering to the tutelary deity of Rome, Jupiter
of the Capitol. But the temple, which had
been burned to the ground in the civil wars, had
not yet been rebuilt, and the princes, anxious
that their gift should not be seen before it was
publicly presented, resolved to carry it back with
them to Syria. Verres, however, had got, no
one knew how, some inkling of the matter, and
he begged Antiochus to let him have a sight of
it. The young prince, who, so far from being
suspicious, was hardly sufficiently cautious, had
it carefully wrapped up, and sent it to the
governor's palace. When he had minutely
inspected it, the messengers prepared to carry
it back. Verres, however, had not seen enough
of it. It clearly deserved more than one
examination. Would they leave it with him
for a time? They left it, suspecting nothing.

Antiochus, on his part, had no apprehensions.
When some days had passed and the candelabrum was not returned, he sent to ask for it.
The governor begged the messenger to come
again the next day. It seemed a strange

request; still the man came again and was
again unsuccessful. The King himself then
waited on the governor and begged him to
return it. Verres hinted, or rather said plainly,
that he should very much like it as a present.
"This is impossible," replied the prince, "the
honor due to Jupiter and public opinion forbid
it. All the world knows that the offering is to
be made, and I cannot go back from my word."
Verres perceived that soft words would be useless, and took at once another line. The King,
he said, must leave Sicily before nightfall. The
public safety demanded it. He had heard of a
piratical expedition which was on its way from
Syria to the province, and that his departure
was necessary. Antiochus had no choice but
to obey; but before he went he publicly protested in the market-place of Syracuse against
the wrong that had been done. His other
valuables, the gold and the jewels, he did not
so much regret; but it was monstrous that he
should be robbed of the gift that he destined
for the altar of the tutelary god of Rome.

The Sicilian cities were not better able to
protect their possessions than were private in-

dividuals. Segesta was a town that had early
ranged itself on the side of the Romans, with
whom its people had a legendary relationship.
(The story was that Æneas on his way to Italy
had left there some of his followers, who were
unwilling any longer to endure the hardships of
the journey.) In early days it had been destroyed by the Carthaginians, who had carried
off all its most valuable possessions, the most
precious being a statue of Diana, a work of great
beauty and invested with a peculiar sacredness.
When Carthage fell, Scipio its conqueror
restored the spoils which had been carried off
from the cities of Sicily. Among other things
Agrigentum had recovered its famous bull of
brass, in which the tyrant Phalaris had burned,
it was said, his victims. Segesta was no less
fortunate than its neighbors, and got back its
Diana. It was set on a pedestal on which
was inscribed the name of Scipio, and became
one of the most notable sights of the island.
It was of a colossal size, but the sculptor had
contrived to preserve the semblance of maidenly
grace and modesty. Verres saw and coveted
it. He demanded it of the authorities of the

town and was met with a refusal. It was easy
for the governor to make them suffer for their
obstinacy. All their imposts were doubled and
more than doubled. Heavy requisitions for men
and money and corn were made upon them.
A still more hateful burden, that of attending
the court and progresses of the governor was
imposed on their principal citizens. This was
a contest which they could not hope to wage
with success. Segesta resolved that the statue
should be given up. It was accordingly carried
away from the town, all the women of the town,
married and unmarried, following it on its
journey, showering perfumes and flowers upon
it, and burning incense before it, till it had
passed beyond the borders of their territory.

If Segesta had its Diana, Tyndaris had its
Mercury ; and this also Verres was resolved to
add to his collection. He issued his orders to
Sopater, chief magistrate of the place, that the
statue was to be taken to Messana. (Messana
being conveniently near to Italy was the place
in which he stored his plunder.) Sopater
refusing was threatened with the heaviest
penalties if it was not done without delay, and

judged it best to bring the matter before the local senate. The proposition was received with shouts of disapproval. Verres paid a second visit to the town and at once inquired what had been done about the statue. He was told that it was impossible. The senate had decreed the penalty of death against any one that touched it. Apart from that, it would be an act of the grossest impiety. "Impiety?" he burst out upon the unlucky magistrates; "penalty of death! senate! what senate? As for you, Sopater, you shall not escape. Give me up the statue or you shall be flogged to death." Sopater again referred the matter to his townsmen and implored them with tears to give way. The meeting separated in great tumult without giving him any answer. Summoned again to the governor's presence, he repeated that nothing could be done. But Verres had still resources in store. He ordered the lictors to strip the man, the chief magistrate, be it remembered, of an important town, and to set him, naked as he was, astride on one of the equestrian statues that adorned the market-place. It was winter; the weather was bitterly cold, with heavy rain.

The pain caused by the naked limbs being thus brought into close contact with the bronze of the statue was intense. So frightful was his suffering that his fellow-townsmen could not bear to see it. They turned with loud cries upon the senate and compelled them to vote that the coveted statue should be given up to the governor. So Verres got his Mercury.

We have a curious picture of the man as he made his progresses from town to town in his search for treasures of art. "As soon as it was spring—and he knew that it was spring not from the rising of any constellation or the blowing of any wind, but simply because he saw the roses— then indeed he bestirred himself. So enduring, so untiring was he that no one ever saw him upon horseback. No—he was carried in a litter with eight bearers. His cushion was of the finest linen of Malta, and it was stuffed with roses. There was one wreath of roses upon his head, and another round his neck, made of the finest thread, of the smallest mesh, and this, too, was full of roses. He was carried in this litter straight to his chamber; and there he gave his audiences."

When spring had passed into summer even such exertions were too much for him. He could not even endure to remain in his official residence, the old palace of the kings of Syracuse. A number of tents were pitched for him at the entrance of the harbor to catch the cool breezes from the sea. There he spent his days and nights, surrounded by troops of the vilest companions, and let the province take care of itself.

Such a governor was not likely to keep his province free from the pirates who, issuing from their fastnesses on the Cilician coast and elsewhere, kept the seaboard cities of the Mediterranean in constant terror. One success, and one only, he seems to have gained over them. His fleet was lucky enough to come upon a pirate ship, which was so overladen with spoil that it could neither escape nor defend itself. News was at once carried to Verres, who roused himself from his feasting to issue strict orders that no one was to meddle with the prize. It was towed into Syracuse, and he hastened to examine his booty. The general feeling was one of delight that a crew of merciless villains had been captured and were about to pay the penalty of their crimes. Verres had far more practical views. Justice might deal as she pleased with the old and useless; the young and able bodied, and all who happened to be handicraftsmen, were too valuable to be given up. His secretaries, his retinue, his son had their share of the prize; six, who happened to be singers, were sent as a present to a friend at Rome. As to the pirate captain himself, no one knew what had become of him. It was a favorite amusement in Sicily to watch the sufferings of a pirate, if the government had had the luck but to catch one, while he was being slowly tortured to death. The people of Syracuse, to whom the pirate captain was only too well known, watched eagerly for the day when he was to be brought out to suffer. They kept an account of those who were brought out to execution, and reckoned them against the number of the crew, which it had been easy to conjecture from the size of the ship. Verres had to correct the deficiency as best he could. He had the audacity to fill the places of the prisoners whom he had sold or given away with Roman citizens, whom on various false pretenses he had thrown into prison. The pirate captain himself was suffered to escape on the payment, it was believed, of a very large sum of money.

But Verres had not yet done with the pirates. It was necessary that some show, at least, of coping with them should be made. There was a fleet, and the fleet must put to sea. A citizen of Syracuse, who had no sort of qualification for the task, but whom Verres was anxious to get out of the way, was appointed to the command. The governor paid it the unwonted attention of coming out of his tent to see it pass. His very dress, as he stood upon the shore, was a scandal to all beholders. His sandals, his purple cloak, his tunic, or under-garment, reaching to his ankles, were thought wholly unsuitable to the dignity of a Roman magistrate. The fleet, as might be expected, was scandalously ill equipped. Its men for the most part existed, as the phrase is, only "on paper." There was the proper complement of names, but of names only. The prœtor drew from the treasury the pay for these imaginary

soldiers and marines, and diverted it into his
own pocket. And the ships were as ill pro-
visioned as they were ill manned. After they
had been something less than five days at sea
they put into the harbor of Pachynus. The
crews were driven to satisfy their hunger on the
roots of the dwarf palm, which grew, and
indeed still grows, in abundance on that spot.
Cleomenes meanwhile was following the example of his patron. He had his tent pitched
on the shore, and sat in it drinking from morning to night. While he was thus employed
tidings were brought that the pirate fleet was
approaching. He was ill prepared for an
engagement. His hope had been to complete
the manning of his ships from the garrison of
the fort. But Verres had dealt with the fort as
he had dealt with the fleet. The soldiers were
as imaginary as the sailors. Still a man of
courage would have fought. His own ship
was fairly well manned, and was of a commanding size, quite able to overpower the light
vessels of the pirates ; and such a crew as there
was was eager to fight. But Cleomenes was as
cowardly as he was incompetent. He ordered

the mast of his ship to be hoisted, the sails to be set, and the cable cut, and made off with all speed. The rest of his fleet could do nothing but follow his example. The pirates gave chase, and captured two of the ships as they fled. Cleomenes reached the port of Helorus, stranded his ship, and left it to its fate. His colleagues did the same. The pirate chief found them thus deserted and burned them. He had then the audacity to sail into the inner harbor of Syracuse, a place into which, we are told, only one hostile fleet, the ill-fated Athenian expedition, three centuries and a half before, had ever penetrated. The rage of the inhabitants at this spectacle exceeded all bounds, and Verres felt that a victim must be sacrificed. He was, of course, himself the chief culprit. Next in guilt to him was Cleomenes. But Cleomenes was spared for the same scandalous reason which had caused his appointment to the command. The other captains, who might indeed have shown more courage, but who were comparatively blameless, were ordered to execution. It seemed all the more necessary to remove them because they could have given inconvenient testimony as to the inefficient condition of the ships.

The cruelty of Verres was indeed as conspicuous as his avarice. Of this, as of his other vices, it would not suit the purpose of this book to speak in detail. One conspicuous example will suffice. A certain Gavius had given offense, how we know not, and had been confined in the disused stone quarries which served for the public prison of Syracuse. From these he contrived to escape, and made his way to Messana. Unluckily for himself, he did not know that Messana was the one place in Sicily where it would not be safe to speak against the governor. Just as he was about to embark for Italy he was heard to complain of the treatment which he had received, and was arrested and brought before the chief magistrate of the town. Verres happened to come to the town the same day, and heard what had happened. He ordered the man to be stripped and flogged in the market-place. Gavius pleaded that he was a Roman citizen and offered proof of his claim. Verres refused to listen, and enraged by the repetition of the plea, actually ordered the man to be crucified. "And set up," he said to his lictors, "set up the cross by the straits. He is a Roman citizen, he says, and he will at least be able to have a view of his native country." We know from the history of St. Paul what a genuine privilege and protection this citizenship was. And Cicero exactly expresses the feeling on the subject in his famous words. "It is a crime to put a Roman citizen in irons; it is positive wickedness to inflict stripes upon him; it is close upon parricide to put him to death; as to crucifying him there is no word for it." And on this crowning act of audacity Verres had the recklessness to venture.

After holding office for three years Verres came back to Rome. The people of Messana, his only friends in the islands, had built a merchantman for him, and he loaded it with his spoils. He came back with a light heart. He knew indeed that the Sicilians would impeach him. His wrong-doings had been too gross, too insolent, for him to escape altogether. But he was confident that he had the means in his hands for securing an acquittal. The men that were to judge him were men of his own order. The senators still retained the privilege which Sulla had given them. ⟩They, and they alone, furnished the juries before whom such causes were tried. Of these senators not a few had a fellow-feeling for a provincial governor accused of extortion and wrong. Some had plundered provinces in the past; others hoped to do so in the future. Many insignificant men who could not hope to obtain such promotion were notoriously open to bribes. And some who would have scorned to receive money, or were too wealthy to be influenced by it, were not insensible to the charms of other gifts—to a fine statue or a splendid picture judiciously bestowed. A few, even more scrupulous, who would not accept such presents for their own halls or gardens, were glad to have such splendid ornaments for the games which they exhibited to the people. Verres came back amply provided with these means of securing his safety. He openly avowed—for indeed he was as frank as he was unscrupulous—that he had trebled his extortions in order that, after leaving a sufficiency for himself, he might have where-

with to win the favor of his judges. It soon
became evident to him that he would need
these and all other help, if he was to escape.
The Sicilians engaged Cicero to plead their
cause. He had been quæstor in a division of
the province for a year six years before, and
had won golden opinions by his moderation
and integrity. And Cicero was a power in the
courts of the law, all the greater because he
had never yet prosecuted, but had kept himself
to what was held the more honorable task
of defending persons accused.[1] Verres secured
Hortensius. He too was a great orator ;
Cicero had chosen him as the model which he
would imitate, and speaks of him as having
been a splendid and energetic speaker, full of
life both in diction and action. At that time,
perhaps, his reputation stood higher than that
of Cicero himself. It was something to have
retained so powerful an advocate ; it would
be still more if it could be contrived that the
prosecutor should be a less formidable person.
And there was a chance of contriving this. A

[1] So Horace compliments a friend on being "the illustrious safeguard of the sad accused."

certain Cæcilius was induced to come forward, and claim for himself, against Cicero, the duty of prosecuting the late governor of Sicily. He too had been a quæstor in the province, and he had quarreled, or he pretended that he had quarreled, with Verres. The first thing there had to be argued before the court, which, like our own, consisted of a presiding judge and a jury, was the question, who was to prosecute, Cicero or Cæcilius, or the two together. Cicero made a great speech, in which he established his own claim. He was the choice of the provincials; the honesty of his rival was doubtful, while it was quite certain that he was incompetent. The court decided in his favor, and he was allowed one hundred and ten days to collect evidence. Verres had another device in store. This time a member of the Senate came forward and claimed to prosecute Verres for misdoings in the province of Achaia in Greece. He wanted one hundred and eight days only for collecting evidence. If this claim should be allowed, the second prosecution would be taken first; of course it was not intended to be serious, and would end in an acquittal. Meanwhile all the available time would have been spent, and the Sicilian affair would have to be postponed till the next year. It was on postponement indeed that Verres rested his hopes. In July Hortensius was elected consul for the following year, and if the trial could only be put off till he had entered upon office, nothing was to be feared. Verres was openly congratulated in the streets of Rome on his good fortune. " I have good news for you," cried a friend ; " the election has taken place and you are acquitted." Another friend had been chosen prætor, and would be the new presiding judge. Consul and prætor between them would have the appointment of the new jurors, and would take care that they should be such as the accused desired. At the same time the new governor of Sicily would be also a friend, and he would throw judicious obstacles in the way of the attendance of witnesses. The sham prosecution came to nothing. The prosecutor never left Italy. Cicero, on the other hand, employed the greatest diligence. Accompanied by his cousin Lucius he visited all the chief cities of Sicily, and collected from them an enormous mass of evidence. In this work he only spent fifty out of the hundred and ten days allotted to him, and was ready to begin long before he was expected.

Verres had still one hope left; and this, strangely enough, sprang out of the very number and enormity of his crimes. The mass of evidence was so great that the trial might be expected to last for a long time. If it could only be protracted into the next year, when his friends would be in office, he might still hope to escape. And indeed there was but little time left. The trial began on the fifth of August. In the middle of the month Pompey was to exhibit some games. Then would come the games called "The Games of Rome," and after this others again, filling up much of the three months of September, October, and November. Cicero anticipated this difficulty. He made a short speech (it could not have lasted more than two hours in delivering), in which he stated the case in outline. He made a strong appeal to the jury. They were themselves on their trial. The eyes of all the world were on them. If they did not do justice on so notorious a criminal they would never be trusted any more. It would be seen that the senators were not fit to administer the law. The law itself was on its trial. The provincials openly declared that if Verres was acquitted, the law under which their governors were liable to be accused had better be repealed. If no fear of a prosecution were hanging over them, they would be content with as much plunder as would satisfy their own wants. They would not need to extort as much more wherewith to bribe their judges. Then he called his witnesses. A marvelous array they were. " From the foot of Mount Taurus, from the shores of the Black Sea, from many cities of the Grecian mainland, from many islands of the Ægean, from every city and market-town of Sicily, deputations thronged to Rome. In the porticoes, and on the steps of the temples, in the area of the Forum, in the colonnade that surrounded it, on the housetops and on the overlooking declivities, were stationed dense and eager crowds of impoverished heirs and their guardians, bankrupt tax-farmers and corn merchants, fathers bewailing their children carried off to the prætor's harem, children mourning for their parents dead in the prætor's dungeons, Greek nobles whose descent was traced to Cecrops or Eurysthenes, or to the great Ionian and Minyan houses, and Phœnicians, whose ancestors had been priests of the Tyrian Melcarth, or claimed kindred with the Zidonian Jah."[1] Nine days were spent in hearing this mass of evidence. Hortensius was utterly overpowered by it. He had no opportunity for displaying his eloquence, or making a pathetic appeal for a noble oppressed by the hatred of the democracy. After a few feeble attempts at cross-examination, he practically abandoned the case. The defendant himself perceived that his position was hopeless. Before the nine days, with their terrible impeachment, had come to an end he fled from Rome.

The jury returned an unanimous verdict of guilty, and the prisoner was condemned to banishment and to pay a fine. The place of banishment (which he was apparently allowed to select outside certain limits) was Marseilles. The amount of the fine we do not know. It certainly was not enough to impoverish him.

[1] Article in "Dictionary of Classical Biography and Mythology," by William Bodham Donne.

Much of the money, and many of the works of art which he had stolen were left to him. These latter, by a singularly just retribution, proved his ruin in the end. After the death of Cicero, Antony permitted the exiles to return. Verres came with them, bringing back his treasures of art, and was put to death because they excited the cupidity of the masters of Rome.

CHAPTER V.

THERE were various courts at Rome for persons accused of various crimes. One judge, for instance, used to try charges of poisoning; another, charges of murder; and, just as is the case among us, each judge had a jury, who gave their verdict on the evidence which they had heard. But this verdict was not, as with us, the verdict of the whole jury, given only if all can be induced to agree, but of the majority. Each juryman wrote his opinion on a little tablet of wood, putting A. (*absolvo*, " I acquit.") if he thought the accused innocent, K. (*condemno*, " I condemn ") if he thought him guilty, and N. L. (*non liquet*, " It is not clear ") if the case seemed suspicious, though there was not enough evidence to convict.

In the year 66 B.C. a very strange trial took

place in the Court of Poison Cases. A certain
Cluentius was accused of having poisoned his
step-father, Oppianicus, and various other persons. Cicero, who was prætor that year (the
prætor was the magistrate next in rank to the
consul), defended Cluentius, and told his client's
whole story.

Cluentius and his step-father were both
natives of Larinum, a town in Apulia, where
there was a famous temple of Mars. A dispute
about the property of this temple caused an
open quarrel between the two men, who had
indeed been enemies for some years. Oppianicus took up the case of some slaves, who
were called *Servants of Mars,* declaring that
they were not slaves at all, but Roman citizens.
This he did, it would seem, because he desired
to annoy his fellow-townsmen, with whom he
was very unpopular. The people of Larinum,
who were very much interested in all that concerned the splendor of their temple services,
resisted the claim, and asked Cluentius to plead
their case. Cluentius consented. While the
cause was going on, it occurred to Oppianicus
to get rid of his opponent by poison. He

employed an agent, and the agent put the matter into the hands of his freedman, a certain Scamander. Scamander tried to accomplish his object by bribing the slave of the physician who was attending Cluentius. The physician was a needy Greek, and his slave had probably hard and scanty fare ; but he was an honest man, and as clever as he was honest. He pretended to accept the offer, and arranged for a meeting. This done, he told the whole matter to his master the physician, and the physician told it again to his patient. Cluentius arranged that certain friends should be present in concealment at the interview between the slave and his tempter. The villain came, and was seized with the poison and a packet of money, sealed with his master's seal, upon him.

Cluentius, who had put up with many provocations from his mother's husband, now felt that his life was in danger, and determined to defend himself. He indicted Scamander for an attempt to poison. The man was found guilty. Scamander's patron (as they used to call a freedman's old master) was next brought

to trial, and with the same result. Last of all
Oppianicus, the chief criminal, was attacked.
Scamander's trial had warned him of his
danger, and he had labored to bring about
the man's acquittal. One vote, and one only,
he had contrived to secure. And to the giver
of this vote, a needy and unprincipled member
of the Senate, he now had recourse. He
went, of course, with a large sum in his hand
—something about five thousand six hundred
pounds of our money. With this the senator—
Staienus by name—was to bribe sixteen out of
the thirty-two jurymen. They were to have
three hundred and fifty pounds apiece for their
votes, and Staienus was to have as much for
his own vote (which would give a majority),
and something over for his trouble. Staienus
conceived the happy idea of appropriating the
whole, and he managed it in this way. He
accosted a fellow-juror, whom he knew to be
as unprincipled as himself. " Bulbus," he said,
"you will help me in taking care that we sha'n't
serve our country for nothing." " You may
count on me," said the man. Staienus went on,
" The defendant has promised three hundred

and fifty pounds to every juror who will vote 'Not Guilty.' You know who will take the money. Secure them, and come again to me." Nine days after, Bulbus came with beaming face to Staienus. "I have got the sixteen in the matter you know of ; and now, where is the money ?" "He has played me false," replied the other ; "the money is not forthcoming. As for myself, I shall certainly vote 'Guilty.'"

The trial came to an end, and the verdict was to be given. The defendant claimed that it should be given by word of mouth, being anxious to know who had earned their money. Staienus and Bulbus were the first to vote. To the surprise of all, they voted "Guilty." Rumors too of foul play had spread about. The two circumstances caused some of the more respectable jurors to hesitate. In the end *five* voted for acquittal, *ten* said "Not Proven," and seventeen "Guilty." Oppianicus suffered nothing worse than banishment, a banishment which did not prevent him from living in Italy, and even in the neighborhood of Rome. The Romans, though they shed blood like water in their civil strife, were singularly lenient in their punishments. Not long afterwards he died.

His widow saw in his death an opportunity of gratifying the unnatural hatred which she had long felt for her son Cluentius. She would accuse him of poisoning his step-father. Her first attempt failed completely. She subjected three slaves to torture, one of them her own, another belonged to the younger Oppianicus, a third the property of the physician who had attended the deceased in his last illness. But the cruelties and tortures extorted no confession from the men. At last the friends whom she had summoned to be present at the inquiry compelled her to desist. Three years afterwards she renewed the attempt. She had taken one of the three tortured slaves into high favor, and had established him as a physician at Larinum. The man committed an audacious robbery in his mistress's house, breaking open a chest and abstracting from it a quantity of silver coin and five pounds weight of gold. At the same time he murdered two of his fellow-slaves, and threw their bodies into the fish-pond. Suspicion fell upon the missing slaves. But when the chest came to be closely examined, the opening was found to be of a very curious kind. A friend remembered that he had lately seen among the miscellaneous articles at an auction a circular saw which would have made just such an opening. It was found that this saw had been bought by the physician. He was now charged with the crime. Thereupon a young lad who had been his accomplice came forward and told the story. The bodies were found in the fish-pond. The guilty slave was tortured. He confessed the deed, and he also confessed, his mistress declared, that he had given poison to Oppianicus at the instance of Cluentius. No opportunity was given for further inquiry. His confession made, the man was immediately executed. Under strong compulsion from his step-mother, the younger Oppianicus now took up the case, and indicted Cluentius for murder. The evidence was very weak, little or nothing beyond the very doubtful confession spoken of above ; but then there was a very violent prejudice against the accused. There had been a suspicion—perhaps more than a suspicion—of foul play in the trial which had ended in the condemnation of Oppianicus. The defendant, men said, might have attempted to bribe the jury, but the plaintiff had certainly done so. It would be a fine thing if he were to be punished even by finding him guilty of a crime which he had not committed.

In defending his client, Cicero relied as much upon the terrible list of crimes which had been proved against the dead Oppianicus as upon any thing else. Terrible indeed it was, as a few specimens from the catalogue will prove.

Among the wealthier inhabitants of Larinum was a certain Dinæa, a childless widow. She had lost her eldest son in the Social War (the war carried on between Rome and her Italian allies), and had seen two others die of disease. Her only daughter, who had been married to Oppianicus, was also dead. Now came the unexpected news that her eldest son was still alive. He had been sold into slavery, and was still working among a gang of laborers on a farm in Gaul. The poor woman called her kinsfolk together and implored them to undertake the task of recovering him. At the same

time she made a will, leaving the bulk of her
property to her daughter's son, the younger
Oppianicus, but providing for the missing man
a legacy of between three and four thousand
pounds. The elder Oppianicus was not disposed to see so large a sum go out of the
family. Dinæa fell ill, and he brought her his
own physician. The patient refused the man's
services ; they had been fatal, she said, to all
her kinsfolk. Oppianicus then contrived to introduce to her a traveling quack from Ancona.
He had bribed the man with about seventeen
pounds of our money to administer a deadly
drug. The fee was large, and the fellow was
expected to take some pains with the business ;
but he was in a hurry ; he had many markets
to visit ; and he gave a single dose which there
was no need to repeat.

Meanwhile Dinæa's kinsfolk had sent two
agents to make inquiries for the missing son.
But Oppianicus had been beforehand with
them. He had bribed the man who had
brought the first news, had learned where he
was to be found, and had caused him to be
assassinated. The agents wrote to their

employers at Larinum, saying that the object
of their search could not be found, Oppianicus
having undoubtedly tampered with the person
from whom information was to be obtained.
This letter excited great indignation at Larinum ; and one of the family publicly declared
in the market-place that he should hold
Oppianicus (who happened to be present) responsible if any harm should be found to have
happened to the missing man. A few days
afterwards the agents themselves returned.
They had found the man, but he was dead.
Oppianicus dared not face the burst of rage
which this news excited, and fled from Larinum.
But he was not at the end of his resources.
The Civil War between Sulla and the party
of Marius (for Marius himself was now dead)
was raging, and Oppianicus fled to the camp
of Metellus Pius, one of Sulla's lieutenants.
There he represented himself as one who had
suffered for the party. Metellus had himself
fought in the Social War, and fought against the
side to which the murdered prisoner belonged.
It was therefore easy to persuade him that the
man had deserved his fate, and that his friends

were unworthy persons and dangerous to the commonwealth. Oppianicus returned to Larinum with an armed force, deposed the magistrates whom the towns-people had chosen, produced Sulla's mandate for the appointment of himself and three of his creatures in their stead, as well as for the execution of four persons particularly obnoxious to him. These four were, the man who had publicly threatened him, two of his kinsfolk, and one of the instruments of his own villainies, whom he now found it convenient to get out of the way.

The story of the crimes of Oppianicus, of which only a small part has been given, having been finished, Cicero related the true circumstances of his death. After his banishment he had wandered about for a while shunned by all his acquaintances. Then he had taken up his quarters in a farmhouse in the Falernian country. From these he was driven away by a quarrel with the farmer, and removed to a small lodging which he had hired outside the walls of Rome. Not long afterwards he fell from his horse, and received a severe injury in his side. His health was already weak, fever came on, he was carried into the city and died after a few days' illness.

Besides the charge of poisoning Oppianicus there were others that had to be briefly dealt with. One only of these needs to be mentioned. Cluentius, it was said, had put poison into a cup of honey wine, with the intention of giving it to the younger Oppianicus. The occasion, it was allowed, was the young man's wedding-breakfast, to which, as was the custom at Larinum, a large company had been invited. The prosecutor affirmed that one of the bridegroom's friends had intercepted the cup on its way, drunk off its contents, and instantly expired. The answer to this was complete. The young man had not instantly expired. On the contrary, he had died after an illness of several days, and this illness had had a different cause. He was already out of health when he came to the breakfast, and he had made himself worse by eating and drinking too freely, " as," says the orator, " young men will do." He then called a witness to whom no one could object, the father of the deceased. " The least suspicion of the guilt of Cluentius would have brought him as a witness against him. Instead of doing this he gives him his support. Read," said Cicero to the clerk, "read his evidence. And you, sir," turning to the father, " stand up a while, if you please, and submit to the pain of hearing what I am obliged to relate. I will say no more about the case. Your conduct has been admirable ; you would not allow your own sorrow to involve an innocent man in the deplorable calamity of a false accusation."

Then came the story of the cruel and shameful plot which the mother had contrived against her son. Nothing would content this wicked woman but that she must herself journey to Rome to give all the help that she could to the prosecution. " And what a journey this was ! " cried Cicero. " I live near some of the towns near which she passed, and I have heard from many witnesses what happened. Vast crowds came to see her. Men, ay, and women too, groaned aloud as she passed by. Groaned at what ? Why, that from the distant town of Larinum, from the very shore of the Upper Sea, a woman was coming with a great retinue and heavy money-bags, coming with the single object of bringing about the ruin of a son who was being tried for his life. In all those crowds there was not a man who did not think that every spot on which she set her foot needed to be purified, that the very earth, which is the mother of us all, was defiled by the presence of a mother so abominably wicked. There was not a single town in which she was allowed to stay; there was not an inn of all the many upon that road where the host did not shun the contagion of her presence. And indeed she preferred to trust herself to solitude and to darkness rather than to any city or hostelry. And now," said Cicero, turning to the woman, who was probably sitting in court, " does she think that we do not all know her schemes, her intrigues, her purposes from day to day? Truly we know exactly to whom she has gone, to whom she has promised money, whose integrity she has endeavored to corrupt with her bribes. Nay, more : we have heard all about the things which she supposes to be a secret, her nightly sacrifice, her wicked prayers, her abominable vows."

He then turned to the son, whom he would

have the jury believe was as admirable as the mother was vile. He had certainly brought together a wonderful array of witnesses to character. From Larinum every grown-up man that had the strength to make the journey had come to Rome to support their fellow-townsman. The town was left to the care of women and children. With these witnesses had come, bringing a resolution of the local senate full of the praises of the accused, a deputation of the senators. Cicero turned to the deputation and begged them to stand up while the resolution was being read. They stood up and burst into tears, which indeed are much more common among the people of 'the south than among us, and of which no one sees any reason to be ashamed. "You see these tears, gentlemen," cried the orator to the jury. "You may be sure, from seeing them, that every member of the senate was in tears also when they passed this resolution." Nor was it only Larinum, but all the chief Samnite towns that had sent their most respected citizens to give their evidence for Cluentius. "Few," said Cicero, "I think, are loved by me as much as he is loved by all these friends."

Cluentius was acquitted. Cicero is said to
have boasted afterwards that he had blinded
the eyes of the jury. Probably his client had
bribed the jury in the trial of his step-father.
That was certainly the common belief, which
indeed went so far as to fix the precise sum
which he paid. " How many miles is your farm
from Rome?" was asked of one of the witnesses
at a trial connected with the case. " Less than
fifty-three," he replied. " Exactly the sum,"
was the general cry from the spectators. The
point of the joke is in the fact that the same
word stood in Latin for the *thousand* paces
which made a mile and the *thousand* coins by
which sums of money were commonly reckoned. Oppianicus had paid forty thousand
for an acquittal, and Cluentius outbid him with
fifty thousand ("less than fifty-three") to secure a verdict of guilty. But whatever we may
think of the guilt or innocence of Cluentius,
there can be no doubt that the cause in which
Cicero defended him was one of the most interesting ever tried in Rome.

CHAPTER VI.

COUNTRY LIFE.

A ROMAN of even moderate wealth—for Cicero was far from being one of the richest men of his time—commonly possessed more country-houses than belong even to the wealthiest of English nobles. One such house at least Cicero inherited from his father. It was about three miles from Arpinum, a little town in that hill country of the Sabines which was the proverbial seat of a temperate and frugal race, and which Cicero describes in Homeric phrase as

"Rough but a kindly nurse of men."

In his grandfather's time it had been a plain farmhouse, of the kind that had satisfied the simpler manners of former days—the days when Consuls and Dictators were content,

their time of office ended, to plow their own
fields and reap their own harvests. Cicero
was born within its walls, for the primitive
fashion of family life still prevailed, and the
married son continued to live in his father's
house. After the old man's death, when the
old-fashioned frugality gave way to a more
sumptuous manner of life, the house was
greatly enlarged, one of the additions being
a library, a room of which the grandfather,
who thought that his contemporaries were like
Syrian slaves, " the more Greek they knew
the greater knaves they were," had never felt
the want; but in which his son, especially in
his later days, spent most of his time. The
garden and grounds were especially delightful,
the most charming spot of all being an island
formed by the little stream Fibrenus. A
description put into the mouth of Quintus,
the younger son of the house, thus depicts it :
" I have never seen a more pleasant spot.
Fibrenus here divides his stream into two of
equal size, and so washes either side. Flow-
ing rapidly by he joins his waters again, having
compassed just as much ground as makes a

convenient place for our literary discussions. This done he hurries on, just as if the providing of such a spot had been his only office and function, to fall into the Liris. Then, like one adopted into a noble family, he loses his own obscurer name. The Liris indeed he makes much colder. A colder stream than this indeed I never touched, though I have seen many. I can scarce bear to dip my foot in it. You remember how Plato makes Socrates dip his foot in Ilissus." Atticus too is loud in his praises. "This, you know, is my first time of coming here, and I feel that I cannot admire it enough. As to the splendid villas which one often sees, with their marble pavements and gilded ceilings, I despise them. And their water-courses, to which they give the fine names of Nile or Euripus, who would not laugh at them when he sees your streams? When we want rest and delight for the mind it is to nature that we must come. Once I used to wonder—for I never thought that there was any thing but rocks and hills in the place— that you took such pleasure in the spot. But now I marvel that when you are away from

Rome you care to be any where but here."
"Well," replied Cicero, "when I get away
from town for several days at a time, I do
prefer this place; but this I can seldom do.
And indeed I love it, not only because it is so
pleasant, so healthy a resort, but also because
it is my native land, mine and my father's too,
and because I live here among the associa-
tions of those that have gone before me."

Other homes he purchased at various times
of his life, as his means permitted. The situation of one of them, at Formiæ near Cape
Caista, was particularly agreeable to him, for
he loved the sea; it amused him as it had
amused, he tells us, the noble friends, Scipio
and Lælius, before him, to pick up pebbles on
the shore. But this part of the coast was a
fashionable resort. Chance visitors were common; and there were many neighbors, some
of whom were far too liberal of their visits.
He writes to Atticus on one occasion from his
Formian villa : "As to composition, to which
you are always urging me, it is absolutely impossible. It is a public-hall that I have here,
not a country-house, such a crowd of people is

there at Formiæ. As to most of them nothing need be said. After ten o'clock they cease to trouble me. But my nearest neighbor is Arrius. The man absolutely lives with me, says that he has given up the idea of going to Rome because he wants to talk philosophy with me. And then, on the other side, there is Sebosus, Catulus' friend, as you will remember. Now what am I to do? I would certainly be off to Arpinum if I did not expect to see you here." In the next letter he repeats the complaints: "Just as I am sitting down to write in comes our friend Sebosus. I had not time to give an inward groan, when Arrius says, 'Good morning.' And this is going away from Rome! I will certainly be off to

'My native hills, the cradle of my race.'"

Still, doubtless, there was a sweetness, the sweetness of being famous and sought after, even in these annoyances. He never ceased to pay occasional visits to Formiæ. It was a favorite resort of his family; and it was there that he spent the last days of his life.

But the country-house which he loved best of all was his villa at Tusculum, a Latin town lying on the slope of Mount Algidus, at such a height above the sea[1] as would make a notable hill in England. Here had lived in an earlier generation Crassus, the orator after whose model the young Cicero had formed his own eloquence ; and Catulus, who shared with Marius the glory of saving Rome from the barbarians ; and Cæsar, an elder kinsman of the Dictator. Cicero's own house had belonged to Sulla, and its walls were adorned with frescoes of that great soldier's victories. For neighbors he had the wealthy Lucullus, and the still more wealthy Crassus, one of the three who ruled Rome when it could no longer rule itself, and, for a time at least, Quintus, his brother. "This," he writes to his friend Atticus, " is the one spot in which I can get some rest from all my toils and troubles."

Though Cicero often speaks of this house of his, he nowhere describes its general arrangements. We shall probably be not far wrong if we borrow our idea of this from the letter in

_____
[1] 2200 feet.

which the younger Pliny tells a friend about one of his own country seats.

" The courtyard in front is plain without being mean. From this you pass into a small but cheerful space inclosed by colonnades in the shape of the letter D. Between these there is a passage into an inner covered court, and out of this again into a handsome hall, which has on every side folding doors or windows equally large. On the left hand of this hall lies a large drawing-room, and beyond that a second of a smaller size, which has one window to the rising and another to the setting sun. Adjoining this is another room of a semicircular shape, the windows of which are so arranged as to get the sun all through the day : in the walls are bookcases containing a collection of authors who cannot be read too often. Out of this is a bedroom which can be warmed with hot air. The rest of this side of the house is appropriated to the use of the slaves and freedmen ; yet most of the rooms are good enough to put my guests into. In the opposite wing is a most elegant bedroom, another which can be used both as bedroom and sitting-room, and a third which has an ante-room of its own, and is so high as to be cool in summer, and with walls so thick that it is warm in winter. Then comes the bath with its cooling room, its hot room, and its dressing chamber. And not far from this again the tennis court, which gets the warmth of the afternoon sun, and a tower which commands an extensive view of the country round. Then there is a granary and a store-room."

This was probably a larger villa than Cicero's, though it was itself smaller than another which Pliny describes. We must make an allowance for the increase in wealth and luxury which a century and a half had brought. Still we may get some idea from it of Cicero's country-house, one point of resemblance certainly being that there was but one floor.

What Cicero says about his "Tusculanum" chiefly refers to its furnishing and decoration, and is to be found for the most part in his letters to Atticus. Atticus lived for many years in Athens and had therefore opportunities of buying works of art and books which did not fall in the way of the busy lawyer and statesman of Rome. But the room which in Cicero's eyes was specially important was one which we may call the lecture-room, and he is delighted when his friend was able to procure some appropriate ornaments for it. "Your *Hermathena*," he writes (the *Hermathena* was a composite statue, or rather a double bust upon a pedestal, with the heads of Hermes and Athene, the Roman Mercury and Minerva) "pleases me greatly. It stands so prettily that the whole lecture-room looks like a votive chapel of the deity. I am greatly obliged to you." He returns to the subject in another letter. Atticus had probably purchased for him another bust of the same kind. "What you write about the *Hermathena* pleases me greatly. It is a most appropriate ornament for my own little 'seat of learning.' Hermes is suitable every where, and Minerva is the special emblem of a lecture-room. I should be glad if you would, as you suggest, find as many more ornaments of the same kind for the place. As for the statues that you sent me before, I have not seen them. They are at my house at Formiæ, whither I am just now thinking of going. I shall remove them all to my place at Tusculum. If ever I shall find myself with more than enough for this I shall begin to ornament the other. Pray keep your books. Don't give up the hope that I may be able to make them mine. If I can only do this I shall be richer than Crassus." And, again, " If you can find any lecture-room ornaments do not neglect to secure them. My Tusculum house is so delightful to me that it is only when I get there that I seem to be satisfied with myself." In another letter we hear something about the prices. He has paid about one hundred and eighty pounds for some statues from Megara which his friend had purchased for him. At the same time he thanks him by anticipation for some busts of Hermes, in which the pedestals were of marble from Pentelicus, and the heads of bronze. They had not come to hand when he next writes : " I am looking for them," he says, " most anxiously ; " and he again urges diligence in looking for such things. " You may trust the length of my purse. This is my special fancy." Shortly after Atticus has found another kind of statue, double busts of Hermes and Hercules, the god of strength ; and Cicero is urgent to have them for his lecture-room. All the same he does not forget the books, for which he is keeping his odds and ends of income, his " little vintages," as he calls them—possibly the money received from a small vineyard attached to his pleasure-grounds. Of books, however, he had an ample supply close at home, of which he could make as much use as he pleased, the splendid library which Lucullus had collected. " When I was at my house in Tusculum," he writes in one of his treatises, " happening to want to make use of some books in the library of the young Lucullus, I went to his villa, to take them out myself, as my custom was. Coming there I found Cato (Cato was the lad's uncle and guardian), of whom, however, then I knew nothing, sitting in the library absolutely surrounded with books of the Stoic writers on philosophy."

When Cicero was banished, the house at Tusculum shared the fate of the rest of his property. The building was destroyed. The furniture, and with it the books and works of art so diligently collected, were stolen or sold. Cicero

thought, and was probably right in thinking, that
the Senate dealt very meanly with him when
they voted him something between four and
five thousand pounds as compensation for his
loss in this respect. For his house at Formiæ
they gave him half as much. We hear of his
rebuilding the house. He had advertised the
contract, he tells us in the same letter in which
he complains of the insufficient compensation.
Some of his valuables he recovered, but we hear
no more of collecting. He had lost heart for it,
as men will when such a disaster has happened to
them. He was growing older too, and the times
were growing more and more troublous. Possibly money was not so plentiful with him as it
had been in earlier days. But we have one noble
monument of the man connected with the
second of his two Tusculum houses. He makes
it the scene of the " Discussions of Tusculum,"
one of the last of the treatises in the writing
of which he found consolation for private and
public sorrows. He describes himself as resort-
ing in the afternoon to his " Academy," and
there discussing how the wise man may rise
superior to the fear of death, to pain and to

sorrow, how he may rule his passions, and find contentment in virtue alone. "If it seems," he says, summing up the first of these discussions, "if it seems the clear bidding of God that we should quit this life [he seems to be speaking of suicide, which appeared to a Roman to be, under certain circumstances, a laudable act], let us obey gladly and thankfully. Let us consider that we are being loosed from prison, and released from chains, that we may either find our way back to a home that is at once everlasting and manifestly our own, or at least be quit forever of all sensation and trouble. If no such bidding come to us, let us at least cherish such a temper that we may look on that day so dreadful to others as full of blessing to us; and let us look on nothing that is ordered for us either by the everlasting gods or by nature, our common mother, as an evil. It is not by some random chance that we have been created. There is beyond all doubt some mighty Power which watches over the race of man, which does not produce a creature whose doom it is, after having exhausted all other woes, to fall at last into the unending woe of death. Rather let us believe that we have in death a haven and refuge prepared for us. I would that we might sail thither with wide-spread sails ; if not, if contrary winds shall blow us back, still we must needs reach, though it may be somewhat late, the haven where we would be. And as for the fate which is the fate of all, how can it be the unhappiness of one ?"

CHAPTER VII.

A GREAT CONSPIRACY.

SERGIUS CATILINE belonged to an ancient family which had fallen into poverty. In the evil days of Sulla, when the nobles recovered the power which they had lost, and plundered and murdered their adversaries, he had shown himself as cruel and as wicked as any of his fellows. Like many others he had satisfied grudges of his own under pretense of serving his party, and had actually killed his brother-in-law with his own hand. These evil deeds and his private character, which was of the very worst, did not hinder him from rising to high offices in the State. He was made first ædile, then prætor, then governor of Africa, a province covering the region which now bears the names of Tripoli and Tunis. At the end of his year of government he returned to Rome, intending to become a candidate for the consul-ship. In this he met with a great disappoint-ment. He was indicted for misgovernment in his province, and as the law did not permit any one who had such a charge hanging over him to stand for any public office, he was compelled to retire. But he soon found, or fancied that he had found, an opportunity of revenging him-self. The two new consuls were found guilty of bribery, and were compelled to resign. One of them, enraged at his disgrace, made com-mon cause with Catiline. A plot, in which not a few powerful citizens were afterwards sus-pected with more or less reason of having joined, was formed. It was arranged that the consuls should be assassinated on the first day of the new year; the day, that is, on which they were to enter on their office. But a rumor of some impending danger got about; on the appointed day the new consuls appeared with a sufficient escort, and the conspirators agreed to postpone the execution of their scheme till an early day in February. This time the secret was better kept, but the impatience of

Catiline hindered the plot from being carried out. It had been arranged that he should take his place in front of the senate-house, and give to the hired band of assassins the signal to begin. This signal he gave before the whole number was assembled. The few that were present had not the courage to act, and the opportunity was lost.

The trial for misgovernment ended in an acquittal, purchased, it was said, by large bribes given to the jurymen and even to the prosecutor, a certain Clodius, of whom we shall hear again, and shall find to have been not one whit better than Catiline himself. A second trial, this time for misdeeds committed in the days of Sulla, ended in the same way. Catiline now resolved on following another course of action. He would take up the character of a friend of the people. He had the advantage of being a noble, for men thought that he was honest when they saw him thus turn against his own order, and, as it seemed, against his own interests. And indeed there was much that he could say, and say with perfect truth, against the nobles. They were corrupt and

profligate beyond all bearing. They sat on
juries and gave false verdicts for money. They
went out to govern provinces, showed themselves horribly cruel and greedy, and then
came home to be acquitted by men who had
done or hoped to do the very same things
themselves. People listened to Catiline when
he spoke against such doings, without remembering that he was just as bad himself. He
had too, just the reputation for strength and
courage that was likely to make him popular.
He had never been a soldier, but he was
known to be very brave, and he had a remarkable power of enduring cold and hunger and
hardships of every kind. On the strength of
the favor which he thus gained, he stood
again for the consulship. In anticipation of
being elected, he gathered a number of men
about him, unsuccessful and discontented like
himself, and unfolded his plans. All debts
were to be wiped out, and wealthy citizens
were to be put to death and their property to
be divided. It was hoped that the consuls at
home, and two at least of the armies in the
provinces, would support the movement. The

first failure was that Catiline was not elected consul, Cicero being chosen unanimously, with Antonius, who had a small majority over Catiline, for his colleague. Enraged at his want of success, the latter now proceeded to greater lengths than ever. He actually raised troops in various parts of Italy, but especially in Etruria, which one Manlius, an old officer in Sulla's army, commanded. He then again became a candidate for the consulship, resolving first to get rid of Cicero, who, he found, met and thwarted him at every turn. Happily for Rome these designs were discovered through the weakness of one of his associates. This man told the secret to a lady, with whom he was in love, and the lady, dismayed at the boldness and wickedness of the plan, communicated all she knew to Cicero.

Not knowing that he was thus betrayed, Catiline set about ridding himself of his great antagonist. Nor did the task seem difficult. The hours both of business and of pleasure in Rome were what we should think inconveniently early. Thus a Roman noble or statesman would receive in the first hours of the

morning the calls of ceremony or friendship
which it is our custom to pay in the afternoon.
It would sometimes happen that early visitors
would find the great man not yet risen. In
these cases he would often receive them in
bed. This was probably the habit of Cicero,
a courteous, kindly man, always anxious to be
popular, and therefore easy of access. On this
habit the conspirators counted. Two of their
number, one of them a knight, the other a
senator, presented themselves at his door
shortly after sunrise on the seventh of November. They reckoned on finding him, not in
the great hall of his mansion, surrounded by
friends and dependents, but in his bed-chamber.
But the consul had received warning of their
coming, and they were refused admittance.
The next day he called a meeting of the Senate in the temple of Jupiter the Stayer, which
was supposed to be the safest place where they
could assemble,

To this meeting Catiline, a member in right
of having filled high offices of state, himself
ventured to come. A tall, stalwart man, manifestly of great power of body and mind, but

with a face pale and wasted by excess, and his eyes haggard and bloodshot, he sat alone in the midst of a crowded house. No man had greeted him when he entered, and when he took his place on the benches allotted to senators who had filled the office of consul, all shrank from him. Then Cicero rose in his place. He turned directly and addressed his adversary. " How long, Catiline," he cried, "will you abuse our patience?" How had he dared to come to that meeting? Was it not enough for him to know how all the city was on its guard against him; how his fellow-senators shrank from him as men shrink from a pestilence? If he was still alive, he owed it to the forbearance of those against whom he plotted; and this forbearance would last so long, and so long only, as to allow every one to be convinced of his guilt. For the present, he was suffered to live, but to live guarded and watched and incapable of mischief. Then the speaker related every detail of the conspiracy. He knew not only every thing that the accomplices had intended to do, but the very days that had been fixed for doing it. Overwhelmed by this knowledge of his plans, Catiline scarcely attempted a defense. He said in a humble voice, " Do not think, Fathers, that I, a noble of Rome, I who have done myself, whose ancestors have done much good to this city, wish to see it in ruins, while this consul, a mere lodger in the place, would save it." He would have said more, but the whole assembly burst into cries of " Traitor ! Traitor ! " and drowned his voice. " My enemies," he cried, " are driving me to destruction. But look ! if you set my house on fire, I will put it out with a general ruin." And he rushed out of the Senate. Nothing, he saw, could be done in Rome ; every point was guarded against him. Late that same night he left the city, committing the management of affairs to Cethegus and Lentulus, and promising to return before long with an army at his back. Halting awhile on his road, he wrote letters to some of the chief senators, in which he declared that for the sake of the public peace he should give up the struggle with his enemies and quietly retire to Marseilles. What he really did was to make his way to the camp of Manlius, where he assumed the usual state of a regular military command. The Senate, on hearing of these doings, declared him to be an outlaw. The consuls were to raise an army; Antonius was to march against the enemy, and Cicero to protect the city.

Meanwhile the conspirators left behind in Rome had been busy. One of the tribes of Gaul had sent deputies to the Capitol to obtain redress for injuries of which they complained. The men had effected little or nothing. The Senate neglected them. The help of officials could only be purchased by heavy bribes. They were now heavily in debt both on their own account and on account of their state, and Lentulus conceived the idea of taking advantage of their needs. One of his freedmen, who had been a trader in Gaul, could speak the language, and knew several of the deputies, opened negotiations with them by his patron's desire. They told him the tale of their wrongs. They could see, they said, no way out of their difficulties. "Behave like men," he answered, "and I will show you a way." He then revealed to them the existence of the conspiracy, explained its objects, and enlarged upon the hopes of success. While he and his friends were busy at Rome, they were to return to Gaul and rouse their fellow-tribesmen to revolt.

There was something tempting in the offer, and the deputies doubted long whether they should not accept it. In the end prudence prevailed. To join the conspiracy and to rebel would be to run a terrible risk for very doubt-ful advantages. On the other hand they might make sure of a speedy reward by telling all they knew to the authorities. This was the course on which they resolved, and they went without loss of time to a Roman noble who was the hereditary " patron " of their tribe. The patron in his turn communicated the intel-ligence to Cicero. Cicero's instructions were that the deputies should pretend to agree to the proposals which had been made to them, and should ask for a written agreement which they might show to their countrymen at home. An agreement was drawn up, signed by Len-tulus and two of his fellow-conspirators, and handed over to the Gauls, who now made preparations to return to their country. Cicero himself tells us in the speech which he delivered next day in the Forum the story of what followed.

"I summoned to my presence two of the prætors on whose courage I knew I could rely, put the whole matter before them, and unfolded my own plans. As it grew dusk they made their way unobserved to the Mulvian Bridge, and posted themselves with their attendants (they had some trusty followers of their own, and I had sent a number of picked swordsmen from my own body-guard), in two divisions in houses on either side of the bridge. About two o'clock in the morning the Gauls and their train, which was very numerous, began to cross the bridge. Our men charged them; swords were drawn on both sides; but before any blood was shed the prætors appeared on the scene, and all was quiet. The Gauls handed over to them the letters which they had upon them with their seals unbroken. These and the deputies themselves were brought to my house. The day was now beginning to dawn. Immediately I sent for the four men whom I knew to be the principal conspirators. They came suspecting nothing, Lentulus, who had been up late the night before writing the letters, being the last to present himself. Some distinguished persons who had assembled at my house wished me to open the letters before laying them before the Senate. If their contents were not what I suspected I should be blamed for having given a great deal of trouble to no purpose. I refused in so important a matter to act on my own responsibility. No one, I was sure, would accuse me of being too careful when the safety of Rome was at stake. I called a meeting of the Senate, and took care that the attendance should be very large. Meanwhile, at the suggestion of the Gauls, I sent a prætor to the house of Cethegus to seize all the weapons that he could find. He brought away a great number of daggers and swords.

"The Senate being now assembled, I brought Vulturcius, one of the conspirators, into the House, promised him a public pardon, and bade him tell all he knew without fear. As soon as the man could speak, for he was terribly frightened, he said, 'I was taking a

letter and a message from Lentulus to Catiline.
Catiline was instructed to bring his forces up
to the walls of the city. They meanwhile
would set it on fire in various quarters, as
had been arranged, and begin a general massacre. He was to intercept the fugitives, and
thus effect a junction with his friends within
the walls.' I next brought the Gauls into the
House. Their story was as follows. ' Lentulus
and two of his companions gave us letters to
our nation. We were instructed to send our
cavalry into Italy with all speed. They would
find a force of infantry. Lentulus told us how
he had learned from Sibylline books that he was
that " third Cornelius " who was the fated ruler
of Rome. The two that had gone before him
were Cicero and Sulla. The year too was the
one which was destined to see the ruin of the
city, for it was the tenth after the acquittal of
the Vestal Virgins, the twentieth after the
burning of the Capitol. After this Cethegus
and the others had a dispute about the time
for setting the city on fire. Lentulus and others
wished to have it done on the feast of Saturn
(December 17th). Cethegus thought that this

was putting it off too long.' I then had the letter brought in. First I showed Cethegus his seal. He acknowledged it. I cut the string. I read the letter. It was written in his own handwriting and was to this effect: he assured the Senate and people of the Gauls that he would do what he had promised to their deputies, and begged them on the other hand to perform what their deputies had undertaken. Cethegus, who had accounted for the weapons found in his house by declaring that he had always been a connoisseur in such things, was overwhelmed by hearing his letter read, and said nothing.

"Manlius next acknowledged his seal and handwriting. A letter from him much to the same effect was read. He confessed his guilt. I then showed Lentulus his letter, and asked him, 'Do you acknowledge the seal?' 'I do,' he answered. 'Yes,' said I, 'it is a well-known device, the likeness of a great patriot, your grandfather. The mere sight of it ought to have kept you from such a crime as this.' His letter was then read. I then asked him whether he had any explanation to give. 'I have nothing to say,' was his first answer. After a while he rose and put some questions to the Gauls. They answered him without any hesitation, and asked him in reply whether he had not spoken to them about the Sibylline books. What followed was the strangest proof of the power of conscience. He might have denied every thing, but he did what no one expected, he confessed ; all his abilities, all his power of speech deserted him. Vulturcius then begged that the letter which he was carrying from Lentulus to Catiline should be brought in and opened. Lentulus was greatly agitated ; still he acknowledged the seal and the handwriting to be his. The letter, which was unsigned, was in these words : *You will know who I am by the messenger whom I send to you. Bear yourself as a man. Think of the position in which you now are, and consider what you must now do. Collect all the help you can, even though it be of the meanest kind.* In a word, the case was made out against them all not only by the seals, the letters, the handwritings, but by the faces of the men, their downcast look, their silence. Their confusion, their stealthy looks at each other were enough, if there had been no other proof, to convict them."

Lentulus was compelled to resign his office of prætor. He and the other conspirators were handed over to certain of the chief citizens, who were bound to keep them in safe custody and to produce them when they were called for.

The lower orders of the capital, to whom Catiline and his companions had made liberal promises, and who regarded his plans, or what were supposed to be his plans, with considerable favor, were greatly moved by Cicero's account of what had been discovered. No one could expect to profit by conflagration and massacre ; and they were disposed to take sides with the party of order. Still there were elements of danger, as there always are in great cities. It was known that a determined effort would be made by the clients of Lentulus, whose family was one of the noblest and wealthiest in Rome, to rescue him from custody. At the same time several of the most powerful nobles were strongly suspected of favoring the revolutionists. Crassus, in particular, the wealthiest

man in Rome, was openly charged with com-
plicity. A certain Tarquinius was brought
before the Senate, having been, it was said,
arrested when actually on his way to Catiline.
Charged to tell all he knew, he gave the same
account as had been given by other witnesses
of the preparations for fire and massacre, and
added that he was the bearer of a special
message from Crassus to Catiline, to the effect
that he was not to be alarmed by the arrest of
Lentulus and the others; only he must march
upon the city without delay, and so rescue the
prisoners and restore the courage of those who
were still at large. The charge seemed incredible to most of those who heard it. Crassus
had too much at stake to risk himself in such
perilous ventures. Those who believed it were
afraid to press it against so powerful a citizen;
and there were many who were under too great
obligations to the accused to allow it, whatever
its truth or falsehood, to be insisted upon. The
Senate resolved that the charge was false, and
that its author should be kept in custody till
he disclosed at whose suggestion he had come
forward. Crassus himself believed that the

consul had himself contrived the whole business, with the object of making it impossible
for him to take the part of the accused. "He
complained to me," says Sallust the historian,
"of the great insult which had thus been put
upon him by Cicero."

Under these circumstances Cicero determined to act with vigor. On the fifth of December
he called a meeting of the Senate, and put it
to the House what should be done with the
prisoners in custody. The consul elect gave
his opinion that they should be put to death.
Cæsar, when his turn came to speak, rose and
addressed the Senate. He did not seek to
defend the accused. They deserved any punishment. Because that was so, let them be dealt
with according to law. And the law was that
no Roman citizen could suffer death except by
a general decree of the people. If any other
course should be taken, men would afterwards
remember not their crimes but the severity
with which they had been treated. Cato followed, giving his voice for the punishment of
death ; and Cicero took the same side. The
Senate, without dividing, voted that the pris-

oners were traitors, and must pay the usual penalty.

The consul still feared that a rescue might be attempted. He directed the officials to make all necessary preparations, and himself conducted Lentulus to prison, the other criminals being put into the charge of the prætors. The prison itself was strongly guarded. In this building, which was situated under the eastern side of the Capitoline Hill, was a pit twelve feet deep, said to have been constructed by King Tullius. It had stone walls and a vaulted stone roof; it was quite dark, and the stench and filth of the place were hideous. Lentulus was hurried into this noisome den, where the executioners strangled him. His accomplices suffered the same fate. The consul was escorted to his house by an enthusiastic crowd. When he was asked how it had fared with the condemned, he answered with the significant words "THEY HAVE LIVED."

The chief conspirator died in a less ignoble fashion. He had contrived to collect about twelve thousand men; but only a fourth part of these were regularly armed; the rest carried hunting spears, pikes, sharpened stakes, any weapon that came to hand. At first he avoided an engagement, hoping to hear news of something accomplished for his cause by the friends whom he had left behind him in Rome. When the news of what had happened on the fifth of December reached him, he saw that his position was desperate. Many who had joined the ranks took the first opportunity of deserting ; with those that remained faithful he made a hurried march to the north-west, hoping to make his way across the Apennines into Hither Gaul. But he found a force ready to bar his way, while Antonius, with the army from Rome, was pressing him from the south. Nothing remained for him but to give battle. Early in the year 62 B.C. the armies met. The rebel leader showed himself that day at his best. No soldier could have been braver, no general more skillful. But the forces arrayed against him were overpowering. When he saw that all was lost, he rushed into the thickest of the fight, and fell pierced with wounds. He was found afterwards far in advance of his men, still breathing and with the same haughty expression on his face which had distinguished him in life. And such was the contagious force of his example that not a single free man of all his followers was taken alive either in the battle or in the pursuit that followed it. Such was the end of a GREAT CONSPIRACY.

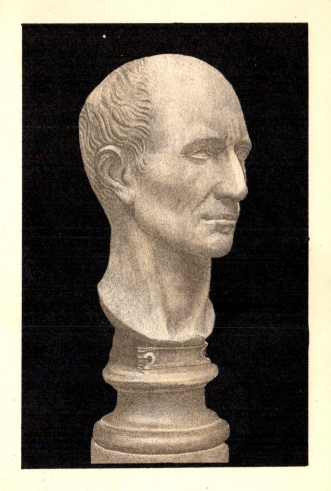

CAIUS JULIUS CÆSAR.

CHAPTER VIII.

CÆSAR.

At eight-and-twenty, Cæsar, who not thirty years later was to die master of Rome, was chiefly known as a fop and a spendthrift. " In all his schemes and all his policy," said Cicero, " I discern the temper of a tyrant ; but then when I see how carefully his hair is arranged, how delicately with a single finger he scratches his head, I cannot conceive him likely to entertain so monstrous a design as overthrowing the liberties of Rome." As for his debts they were enormous. He had contrived to spend his own fortune and the fortune of his wife ; and he was more than three hundred thousand pounds in debt. This was before he had held any public office ; and office, when he came to hold it, certainly did not improve his position.

He was appointed one of the guardians of the Appian Way (the great road that led southward from Rome, and was the route for travelers to Greece and the East). He spent a great sum of money in repairs. His next office of ædile was still more expensive. Expensive it always was, for the ædile, besides keeping the temples and other public buildings in repair (the special business signified by his name), had the management of the public games. An allowance was made to him for his expenses from the treasury, but he was expected, just as the Lord Mayor of London is expected, to spend a good deal of his own money. Cæsar far outdid all his predecessors. At one of the shows which he exhibited, three hundred and twenty pairs of gladiators fought in the arena; and a gladiator, with his armor and weapons, and the long training which he had to undergo before he could fight in public, was a very expensive slave. The six hundred and forty would cost, first and last, not less than a hundred pounds apiece, and many of them, perhaps a third of the whole number, would be killed in the

course of the day. Nor was he content with
the expenses which were more or less necessary. He exhibited a great show of wild
beasts in memory of his father, who had died
nearly twenty years before. The whole furniture of the theater, down to the very stage,
was made on this occasion of solid silver.

For all this seeming folly, there were
those who discerned thoughts and designs
of no common kind. Extravagant expenditure was of course an usual way of winning
popular favors. A Roman noble bought
office after office till he reached one that
entitled him to be sent to govern a province.
In the plunder of the province he expected
to find what would repay him all that he had
spent and leave a handsome sum remaining.
Cæsar looked to this end, but he looked also to
something more. He would be the champion
of the people, and the people would make him
the greatest man at Rome. This had been the
part played by Marius before him; and he
determined to play it again. The name of
Marius had been in ill repute since the victory
of his great rival, Sulla, and Cæsar determined

to restore it to honor. He caused statues of this great man to be secretly made, on which were inscribed the names of the victories by which he had delivered Rome from the barbarians. On the morning of the show these were seen, splendid with gilding, upon the height of the Capitol. The first feeling was a general astonishment at the young magistrate's audacity. Then the populace broke out into expressions of enthusiastic delight ; many even wept for joy to see again the likeness of their old favorite ; all declared that Cæsar was his worthy successor. The nobles were filled with anger and fear. Catulus, who was their leader, accused Cæsar in the Senate. " This man," he said, " is no longer digging mines against his country, he is bringing battering-rams against it." The Senate, however, was afraid or unwilling to act. As for the people, it soon gave the young man a remarkable proof of its favor. What may be called the High Priesthood became vacant. It was an honor commonly given to some aged man who had won victories abroad and borne high honors at home. Such competitors there were on this occasion, Catulus being one of them. But Cæsar, though far below the age at which such offices were commonly held, determined to enter the lists. He refused the heavy bribe by which Catulus sought to induce him to withdraw from the contest, saying that he would raise a greater sum to bring it to a successful end. Indeed, he staked all on the struggle. When on the day of election he was leaving his house, his mother followed him to the door with tears in her eyes. He turned and kissed her, "Mother," he said, "to-day you will see your son either High Priest or an exile."

The fact was that Cæsar had always shown signs of courage and ambition, and had always been confident of his future greatness. Now that his position in the country was assured men began to remember these stories of his youth. In the days when Sulla was master of Rome, Cæsar had been one of the very few who had ventured to resist the great man's will. Marius, the leader of the party, was his uncle, and he had himself married the daughter of Cunia, another of the popular leaders. This wife Sulla ordered him to divorce, but he flatly refused. For some time his life was in danger; but Sulla was induced to spare it, remarking, however, to friends who interceded for him, on the ground that he was still but a boy, "You have not a grain of sense, if you do not see that in this boy there is the material for many Mariuses." The young Cæsar found it safer to leave Italy for a time. While traveling in the neighborhood of Asia Minor he fell into the hands of the pirates, who were at that time the terror of all the Eastern Mediterranean. His first proceeding was to ask them how much they wanted for his ransom. "Twenty talents," (about five thousand pounds) was their answer. "What folly!" he said, "you don't know whom you have got hold of. You shall have fifty." Messengers were sent to fetch the money, and Cæsar, who was left with a friend and a couple of slaves, made the best of the situation. If he wanted to go to sleep he would send a message commanding his captors to be silent. He joined their sports, read poems and speeches to them, and roundly abused them as ignorant barbarians if they failed to applaud. But his most telling joke was threatening to hang them.

The men laughed at the free-spoken lad, but were not long in finding that he was in most serious earnest. In about five weeks' time the money arrived and Cæsar was released. He immediately went to Miletus, equipped a squadron, and returning to the scene of his captivity, found and captured the greater part of the band. Leaving his prisoners in safe custody at Pergamus, he made his way to the governor of the province, who had in his hands the power of life and death. But the governor, after the manner of his kind, had views of his own. The pirates were rich and could afford to pay handsomely for their lives. He would consider the case, he said. This was not at all to Cæsar's mind. He hastened back to Pergamus, and, taking the law into his own hands, crucified all the prisoners.

This was the cool and resolute man in whom the people saw their best friend and the nobles their worst enemy. These last seemed to see a chance of ruining him when the conspiracy of Catiline was discovered and crushed. He was accused, especially by Cato, of having been an accomplice; and when he left the Senate after

the debate in which he had argued against putting the arrested conspirators to death, he was
mobbed by the gentlemen who formed Cicero's
body-guard, and was even in danger of his life.
But the formal charge was never pressed; indeed it was manifestly false, for Cæsar was too
sure of the favor of the people to have need
of conspiring to win it. The next year he was
made prætor, and after his term of office was
ended, governor of Further Spain. The old
trouble of debt still pressed upon him, and he
could not leave Rome till he had satisfied the
most pressing of his creditors. This he did by
help of Crassus, the richest man in Rome, who
stood security for nearly two hundred thous-
and pounds. To this time belong two anecdotes
which, whether true or no, are curiously characteristic of his character. He was passing, on
the way to his province, a town that had a
particularly mean and poverty-stricken look.
One of his companions remarked, "I dare say
there are struggles for office even here, and
jealousies and parties." "Yes," said Cæsar;
"and indeed, for myself, I would sooner be
the first man here than the second in Rome."

Arrived at his journey's end, he took the opportunity of a leisure hour to read the life of Alexander. He sat awhile lost in thought, then burst into tears. His friends inquired the cause. "The cause?" he replied. "Is it not cause enough that at my age Alexander had conquered half the world, while I have done nothing?" Something, however, he contrived to do in Spain. He extended the dominion of Rome as far as the Atlantic, settled the affairs of the provincials to their satisfaction, and contrived at the same time to make money enough to pay his debts. Returning to Rome when his year of command was ended, he found himself in a difficulty. He wished to have the honor of a triumph (a triumph was a procession in which a victorious general rode in a chariot to the Capitol, preceded and followed by the spoils and prisoners taken in his campaigns), and he also wished to become a candidate for the consulship. But a general who desired a triumph had to wait outside the gates of the city till it was voted to him, while a candidate for the consulship must lose no time in beginning to canvass the people. Cæsar, having to make his choice between the two, preferred power to show. He stood for the consulship, and was triumphantly elected.

Once consul he made that famous Coalition which is commonly called the First Triumvirate. Pompey was the most famous soldier of the day, and Crassus, as has been said before, the richest man. These two had been enemies, and Cæsar reconciled them ; and then the three together agreed to divide power and the prizes of power between them. Cæsar would have willingly made Cicero a fourth, but he refused, not, perhaps, without some hesitation. He did more ; he ventured to say some things which were not more agreeable because they were true of the new state of things. This the three masters of Rome were not willing to endure, and they determined that this troublesome orator should be put out of the way. They had a ready means of doing it. A certain Clodius, of whom we shall hear more hereafter, felt a very bitter hatred against Cicero, and by way of putting himself in a position to injure him, and to attain other objects of his own, sought to be made tribune. But there was a great obstacle in the way. The tribunes were tribunes of the *plebs*, that is, of the commons, whose interests they were supposed specially to protect ; while Clodius was a noble—indeed, a noble of nobles—belonging as he did to that great Claudian House which was one of the oldest and proudest of Roman families. The only thing to be done was to be adopted by some plebeian. But here, again, there were difficulties. The law provided that an adoption should be real, that the adopter should be childless and, old enough to be the father of his adopted son. The consent of the priests was also necessary. This consent was never asked, and indeed never could have been given, for the father was a married man, had children of his own, and was not less than fifteen years younger than his new son. Indeed the bill for making the adoption legal had been before the people for more than a year without making any progress. The Three now took it up to punish Cicero for his presumption in opposing them ; and under its new promoters it was passed in a single day, being proposed at noon and made law by three o'clock in the afternoon.

What mischief Clodius was thus enabled to work against Cicero we shall hear in the next chapter but one.

His consulship ended, Cæsar received a substantial prize for his services, the government of the province of Gaul for five years. Before he left Italy to take up his command, he had the satisfaction of seeing Cicero driven into banishment. That done, he crossed the Alps. The next nine years (for his government was prolonged for another period when the first came to an end) he was engaged in almost incessant war, though still finding time to manage the politics of Rome. The campaigns which ended in making Gaul from the Alps to the British Channel, and from the Atlantic to the Rhine, a Roman possession, it is not within my purpose to describe. Nevertheless, it may be interesting to say a few words about his dealings with our own island. In his first expedition, in the summer of 55 B.C., he did little more than effect a landing on the coast, and this not without considerable loss. In the next, made early in the following year, he employed a force of more than forty thousand men, con-

A British Chieftain.

veyed in a flotilla of eight hundred ships. This
time the Britons did not venture to oppose
his landing; and when they met him in the
field, as he marched inward, they were invariably
defeated. They then changed their tactics and
retired before him, laying waste the country as
they went. He crossed the Thames some little
way to the westward of where London now
stands, received the submission of one native
tribe, and finally concluded a peace with the
native leader Cassivelaunus, who gave hostages
and promised tribute. The general result of ten
years' fighting was to add a great province to
the empire at the cost of a horrible amount of
bloodshed, of the lives, as some say, of two mil-
lions of men, women, and children (for Cæsar,
though not positively cruel, was absolutely careless of suffering), and to leave the conqueror
master of the Roman world. The coalition indeed was broken up, for Crassus had perished in
the East, carrying on a foolish and unprovoked
war with the Parthians, and Pompey had come
to fear and hate his remaining rival. But Cæsar
was now strong enough to do without friends,
and to crush enemies. The Senate vainly

commanded him to disperse his army by a certain day, on pain of being considered an enemy of the country. He continued to advance till he came to the boundaries of Italy, a little river, whose name, the Rubicon, was then made famous forever, which separated Cisalpine Gaul from Umbria. To cross this was practically to declare war, and even the resolute Cæsar hesitated awhile. He thought his course over by himself; he even consulted his friends. He professed himself pained at the thought of the war of which his act would be the beginning, and of how posterity would judge his conduct. Then with the famous words, "The die is cast," he plunged into the stream. Pompey fled from Rome and from Italy. Cæsar did not waste an hour in pursuing his success. First making Italy wholly his own, he marched into Spain, which was Pompey's stronghold, and secured it. Thence he returned to Rome, and from Rome again made his way into Macedonia, where Pompey had collected his forces. The decisive battle was fought at Pharsalia in Thessaly; for though the remnants of Pompey's party held out, the issue of the war was never doubtful after that day.

Returning to Rome (for of his proceedings in Egypt and elsewhere there is no need to speak), he used his victory with as much mercy as he had shown energy in winning it. To Cicero he showed not only nothing of malice, but the greatest courtesy and kindness. He had written to him from Egypt, telling him that he was to keep all his dignities and honors; and he had gone out of his way to arrange an interview with him, and he even condescended to enter into a friendly controversy. Cicero had written a little treatise about his friend Cato; and as Cato had been the consistent adversary of Cæsar, and had killed himself rather than fall into the hands of the master of Rome, it required no little good nature in Cæsar to take it in good part. He contented himself with writing an answer, to which he gave the title of *Anti-Cato*, and in which, while he showed how useless and unpractical the policy of Cato had been, he paid the highest compliments to the genius and integrity of the man. He even conferred upon Cicero the distinguished honor of a visit; which the host thus describes in a letter to Atticus. "What a formidable guest I have had! Still, I am not sorry; for all went off very well. On December 8th he came to Philippus' house in the evening. (Philippus was his brother-in-law.) The villa was so crammed with troops that there was scarcely a chamber where the great man himself could dine. I suppose there were two thousand men. I was really anxious what might happen next day. But Barba Cassius came to my help, and gave me a guard. The camp was pitched in the park; the house was strictly guarded. On the 19th he was closeted with Philippus till one o'clock in the afternoon. No one was admitted. He was going over accounts with Balbus, I fancy. After this he took a stroll on the shore. Then came the bath. He heard the epigram to Mamurra, (a most scurrilous epigram by Catullus), and betrayed no annoyance. He dressed for dinner and sat down. As he was under a course of medicine, he ate and drank without apprehension and in the pleasantest humor. The entertainment was sumptuous and elaborate;

and not only this, but well cooked and seasoned
with good talk. The great man's attendants
also were most abundantly entertained in three
other rooms. The inferior freedmen and the
slaves had nothing to complain of; the superior kind had an even elegant reception.
Not to say more, I showed myself a genial
host. Still he was not the kind of guest to
whom we would say, 'My very dear sir, you
will come again, I hope, when you are this
way next time.' There was nothing of importance in our conversation, but much literary
talk. What do you want to know? He was
gratified and seemed pleased to be with me.
He told me that he should be one day at Baiæ,
and another at Puteoli."

Within three months this remarkable career
came to a sudden and violent end. There
were some enemies whom all Cæsar's clemency and kindness had not conciliated. Some
hated him for private reasons of their own,
some had a genuine belief that if he could
be put out of the way, Rome might yet
again be a free country. The people too,
who had been perfectly ready to submit to

the reality of power, grew suspicious of some of its outward signs.   The name of King had been hateful at Rome since the last bearer of it, Tarquin the Proud, had been driven out nearly seven centuries before.   There were now injudicious friends, or, it may be, judicious enemies, who were anxious that Cæsar should assume it.   The prophecy was quoted from the books of the Sibyl, that Rome might conquer the Parthians if she put herself under the command of a king; otherwise she must fail.   On the strength of this Cæsar was saluted by the title of King as he was returning one day from Alba to the Capitol.   The populace made their indignation manifest, and he replied, " I am no king, only Cæsar;" but it was observed that he passed on with a gloomy air.   He bore himself haughtily in the Senate, not rising to acknowledge the compliments paid to him.   At the festival of the Lupercalia, as he sat looking on at the sports in a gilded chair and clad in a triumphal robe, Antony offered him a crown wreathed with bay leaves.   Some applause followed; it was not general, however, but manifestly got up for

the occasion. Cæsar put the crown away, and
the shout that followed could not be misunder-
stood. It was offered again, and a few applauded as before, while a second rejection
drew forth the same hearty approval. His
statues were found with crowns upon them.
These two tribunes removed, and at the
same time ordered the imprisonment of the
men who had just saluted him as king. The
people were delighted, but Cæsar had them
degraded from their office. The general dis-
satisfaction thus caused induced the conspirators to proceed. Warnings, some of which we
may suppose to have come from those who
were in the secret, were not wanting. By
these he was wrought upon so much that he
had resolved not to stir from his house on the
day which he understood was to be fatal to
him ; but Decimus Brutus, who was in the
plot, dissuaded him from his purpose. The
scene that followed may be told once again in
the words in which Plutarch describes it : " Arte-
mídoros, of Cnidus, a teacher of Greek, who
had thus come to be intimate with some of the
associates of Brutus, had become acquainted to

a great extent with what was in progress, and had drawn up a statement of the information which he had to give. Seeing that Cæsar gave the papers presented to him to the slaves with him, he came up close and said, 'Cæsar, read this alone and that quickly : it contains matters that nearly concern yourself.' Cæsar took it, and would have read it, but was hindered by the crowd of persons that thronged to salute him. Keeping it in his hand, he passed into the House. In the place to which the Senate had been summoned stood a statue of Pompey. Cassius is said to have looked at it and silently invoked the dead man's help, and this though he was inclined to the skeptical tenets of Epicurus. Meanwhile Antony, who was firmly attached to Cæsar and a man of great strength, was purposely kept in conversation outside the senate-house by Decimus Brutus. As Cæsar entered, the Senate rose to greet him. Some of the associates of Brutus stood behind his chair; others approached him in front, seemingly joining their entreaties to those which Cimber Tullius was addressing to him on behalf of his brother. He sat down, and rejected the petition with a gesture of disapproval at their urgency. Tullius then seized his toga with both hands and dragged it from his neck. This was the signal for attack. Casca struck him first on the neck. The wound was not fatal, nor even serious, so agitated was the striker at dealing the first blow in so terrible a deed. Cæsar turned upon him, seized the dagger, and held it fast, crying at the same time in Latin, ' Casca, thou villain, what art thou about ?' while Casca cried in Greek to his brother, ' Brother, help !' Those senators who were not privy to the plot were overcome with horror. They could neither cry nor help : they dared not even speak. The conspirators were standing round Cæsar each with a drawn sword in his hand ; whithersoever he turned his eyes he saw a weapon ready to strike, and he struggled like a wild beast among the hunters. They had agreed that every one should take a part in the murder, and Brutus, friend as he was, could not hold back. The rest, some say, he struggled with, throwing himself hither and thither, and crying aloud ; but as soon as he saw Brutus with a drawn sword in his hand, he wrapped his head in his toga and ceased to resist, falling, whether by chance or by compulsion from the assassins, at the pedestal of Pompey's statue. He is said to have received three-and-twenty wounds. Many of his assailants struck each other as they aimed repeated blows at his body." His funeral was a remarkable proof of his popularity. The pit in which the body was to be burned was erected in the Field of Mars. In the Forum was erected a gilded model of the temple of Mother Venus. (Cæsar claimed descent through Æneas from this goddess.) Within this shrine was a couch of ivory, with coverlets of gold and purple, and at its head a trophy with the robe which he had worn when he was assassinated. High officers of state, past and present, carried the couch into the Forum. Some had the idea of burning it in the chapel of Jupiter in the Capitol, some in Pompey's Hall (where he was killed). Of a sudden two men, wearing swords at their side, and each carrying two javelins, came forward and set light to it with waxen torches which they held in their hands. The crowd of bystanders hastily piled up a heap of dry brushwood, throwing on it the hustings, the benches, and any thing that had been brought as a present. The flute players and actors threw off the triumphal robes in which they were clad, rent them, and threw them upon the flames, and the veterans added the decorations with which they had come to attend the funeral, while mothers threw in the ornaments of their children.

The doors of the building in which the murder was perpetrated were blocked up so that it never could be entered again. The day (the 15th of March) was declared to be accursed. No public business was ever to be done upon it.

These proceedings probably represented the popular feeling about the deed, for Cæsar, in addition to the genius which every one must have recognized, had just the qualities which make men popular. He had no scruples, but then he had no meannesses. He incurred enormous debts with but a faint chance of paying them—no chance, we may say, except by the robbery of others. He laid his hands upon what he wanted, taking for instance three thousand pounds weight of gold from the treasury of the Capitol and leaving gilded brass in its stead ; and he plundered the unhappy Gauls without remorse. But then he was as free in giving as he was unscrupulous in taking. He had the personal courage, too, which is one of the most attractive of all qualities. Again and again in battle he turned defeat into victory. He would lay hold of the fugitives as they ran, seize them by the throat, and get them by main force face to face with the foe. Crossing the Hellespont after the battle of Pharsalia in a small boat, he met two of the enemy's ships. Without hesitation he discovered himself, called upon them to surrender, and was obeyed. At Alexandria he was surprised by a sudden sally of the besieged, and had to leap into the harbor. He swam two hundred paces to the nearest ship, lifting a manuscript in his left hand to keep it out of the water, and holding his military cloak in his teeth, for he would not have the enemy boast of securing any spoil from his person.

He allowed nothing to stand in his way. If it suited his policy to massacre a whole tribe, men, women, and children, he gave the order without hesitation, just as he recorded it afterwards in his history without a trace of remorse or regret. If a rival stood in his way he had him removed, and was quite indifferent as to how the removal was effected. But his object gained, or wherever there was no object in question, he could be the kindest and gentlest of men. A friend with whom he was traveling was seized with sudden illness. Cæsar gave up at once to him the only chamber in the little inn, and himself spent the night in the open air. His enemies he pardoned with singular facility, and would even make the first advances. Political rivals, once rendered harmless, were admitted to his friendship, and even promoted to honor ; writers who had assailed him with the coarsest abuse he invited to his table.

Of the outward man this picture has reached us. " He is said to have been remarkably tall, with a light complexion and well-shaped limbs. His face was a little too full ; his eyes black and brilliant. His health was excellent, but towards the latter end of his life he was subject to fainting fits and to frightful dreams at night. On two occasions also, when some public business was being transacted, he had epileptic fits. He was very careful of his personal appearance, had his hair and beard scrupulously cut and shaven.

He was excessively annoyed at the disfigurement of baldness, which he found was made the subject of many lampoons. It had become his habit, therefore, to bring up his scanty locks over his head; and of all the honors decreed to him by the Senate and people, none was more welcome to him than that which gave him the right of continually wearing a garland of bay."

He was wonderfully skillful in the use of arms, an excellent swimmer, and extraordinarily hardy. On the march he would sometimes ride, but more commonly walk, keeping his head uncovered both in rain and sunshine. He traveled with marvelous expedition, traversing a hundred miles in a day for several days together; if he came to a river he would swim it, or sometimes cross it on bladders. Thus he would often anticipate his own messengers. For all this he had a keen appreciation of pleasure, and was costly and even luxurious in his personal habits. He is said, for instance, to have carried with him a tesselated pavement to be laid down in his tent throughout his campaign in Gaul.

CNÆUS POMPEIUS MAGNUS.

CHAPTER IX.

POMPEY.

At an age when Cæsar was still idling away
his time, Pompey had achieved honors such
as the veteran generals of Rome were accustomed to regard as the highest to which they
could aspire. He had only just left, if indeed
he had left, school, when his father took him
to serve under him in the war against the
Italian allies of Rome. He was not more than
nineteen when he distinguished himself by
behaving in circumstances of great difficulty
and danger with extraordinary prudence and
courage. The elder Pompey, Strabo "the
squint-eyed," as his contemporaries called him,
after their strange fashion of giving nicknames
from personal defects, and as he was content
to call himself, was an able general, but hated

for his cruelty and avarice. The leaders of the opposite faction saw an opportunity of getting rid of a dangerous enemy and of bringing over to their own side the forces which he commanded. Their plan was to assassinate the son as he slept, to burn the father in his tent, and at the same time to stir up a mutiny among the troops. The secret, however, was not kept. A letter describing the plot was brought to the young Pompey as he sat at dinner with the ringleader. The lad showed no sign of disturbance, but drank more freely than usual, and pledged his false friend with especial heartiness. He then rose, and after putting an extra guard on his father's tent, composed himself to sleep, but not in his bed. The assassins stabbed the coverlet with repeated blows, and then ran to rouse the soldiers to revolt. The camp was immediately in an uproar, and the elder Pompey, though he had been preserved by his son's precautions, dared not attempt to quell it. The younger man was equal to the occasion. Throwing himself on his face in front of the gate of the camp, he declared that if his comrades were determined to desert to the enemy, they must pass over his dead body. His entreaties prevailed, and a reconciliation was effected between the general and his troops.

Not many weeks after this incident the father died, struck, it was said, by lightning, and Pompey became his own master. It was not long before he found an opportunity of gaining still higher distinction. The civil war still continued to rage, and few did better service to the party of the aristocrats than Pompey. Others were content to seek their personal safety in Sulla's camp ; Pompey was resolved himself to do something for the cause. He made his way to Picenum, where his family estates we e situated and where his own influence was great, and raised three legions (nearly twenty thousand men), with all their commissariat and transport complete, and hurried to the assistance of Sulla. Three of the hostile generals sought to intercept him. He fell with his whole force on one of them, and crushed him, carrying off, besides his victory, the personal distinction of having slain in single combat the champion of the opposing force. The towns by which he passed eagerly hailed him as their deliverer. A second commander who ventured to encounter him found himself deserted by his army and was barely able to escape; a third was totally routed. Sulla received his young partisan, who was not more than twenty-three years of age, with distinguished honors, even rising from his seat and uncovering at his approach.

During the next two years his reputation continued to increase. He won victories in Gaul, in Sicily, and in Africa. As he was returning to Rome after the last of these campaigns, the great Dictator himself headed the crowd that went forth to meet him, and saluted him as Pompey the Great, a title which he continued to use as his family name.[1] But there was a further honor which the young general was anxious to obtain, but Sulla was unwilling to grant, the supreme glory of a triumph. "No one," he said, "who was not or had not been consul, or at least prætor, could triumph. The first of the Scipios, who

---

[1] *Pompeius* was the name of his house (*gens*), *Strabo* had been the name of his family (*familia*). This he seems to have disused, assuming *Magnus* in its stead.

had won Spain from the Carthaginians, had not asked for this honor because he wanted this qualification. Was it to be given to a beardless youth, too young even to sit in the Senate?" But the beardless youth insisted. He even had the audacity to hint that the future belonged not to Sulla but to himself. "More men," he said, "worship the rising than the setting sun." Sulla did not happen to catch the words, but he saw the emotion they aroused in the assembly, and asked that they should be repeated to him. His astonishment permitted him to say nothing more than "Let him triumph! Let him triumph." And triumph he did, to the disgust of his older rivals, whom he intended, but that the streets were not broad enough to allow of the display, still further to affront by harnessing elephants instead of horses to his chariot.

Two years afterwards he met an antagonist more formidable than any he had yet encountered. Sertorius, the champion at once of the party of the people and of the native tribes of Spain, was holding out against the government of Rome. The veteran leader professed a great contempt for his young adversary, "I should whip the boy," he said, "if I were not afraid of the old woman" (meaning Pompey's colleague). But he took good care not to underrate him in practice, and put forth all his skill in dealing with him. Pompey's first campaign against him was disastrous; the successes of the second were checkered by some serious defeats. For five years the struggle continued, and seemed little likely to come to an end, when Sertorius was assassinated by his second in command, Perpenna. Perpenna was unable to wield the power which he had thus acquired, and was defeated and taken prisoner by Pompey. He endeavored to save his life by producing the correspondence of Sertorius. This implicated some of the most distinguished men in Rome, who had held secret communications with the rebel leader and had even invited him over into Italy. With admirable wisdom Pompey, while he ordered the instant execution of the traitor, burned the letters unread.

Returning to Italy he was followed by his usual good fortune. That country had been suffering cruelly from a revolt of the slaves, which the Roman generals had been strangely slow in suppressing. Roused to activity by the tidings of Pompey's approach, Crassus, who was in supreme command, attacked and defeated the insurgent army. A considerable body, however, contrived to escape, and it was this with which Pompey happened to fall in, and which he completely destroyed. " Crassus defeated the enemy," he was thus enabled to boast, " but I pulled up the war by the roots." No honors were too great for a man at once so skillful and so fortunate (for the Romans had always a great belief in a general's good fortune). On the 31st of December, B. C. 71, being still a simple gentleman—that is, having held no civil office in the State—he triumphed for the second time, and on the following day, being then some years below the legal age, and having held none of the offices by which it was usual to mount to the highest dignity in the commonwealth, he entered on his first consulship, Crassus being his colleague.

Still he had not yet reached the height of his glory. During the years that followed his consulship, the pirates who infested the Mediterranean had become intolerable. Issuing, not as was the case in after times, from the harbors of Northern Africa, but from fastnesses in the southern coast of Asia Minor, they plundered the more civilized regions of the West, and made it highly dangerous to traverse the seas either for pleasure or for gain. It was impossible to transport the armies of Rome to the provinces except in the winter, when the pirates had retired to their strongholds. Even Italy itself was not safe. The harbor of Caieta with its shipping, was burned under the very eye of the prætor. From Misenum the pirates carried off the children of the admiral who had the year before led an expedition against them. They even ventured not only to blockade Ostia, the harbor of Rome, and almost within sight of the city, but to capture the fleet that was stationed there. They were especially insulting to Roman citizens. If a prisoner claimed to be such—and the claim generally insured protection—they would pretend the greatest penitence and alarm, falling on their knees before him, and entreating his pardon. Then they would put shoes on his feet, and robe him in a citizen's garb. Such a mistake, they would say, must not happen again. The end of their jest was to make him "walk the plank," and with the sarcastic permission to depart unharmed, they let down a ladder into the sea, and compelled him to descend, under penalty of being still more summarily thrown overboard. Men's eyes began to be turned on Pompey, as the leader who had been prosperous in all his undertakings. In 67 B. C. a law was proposed appointing a commander (who, however, was not named), who should have absolute power for three years over the sea as far as the Pillars of Hercules (the Straits of Gibraltar), and the coast for fifty miles inland, and who should be furnished with two hundred ships, as many soldiers and sailors as he wanted, and more than a million pounds in money. The nobles were furious in their opposition, and prepared to prevent by force the passing of this law. The proposer narrowly escaped with his life, and Pompey himself was threatened. "If you will be another Romulus, like Romulus you shall die" (one form of the legend of Rome's first king represented him as having been torn to pieces by the senators.) But all resistance was unavailing. The new command was created, and of course bestowed upon Pompey. The price of corn, which had risen to a famine height in Rome, fell immediately the appointment was made. The result, indeed, amply justified the choice. The new general made short work of the task that had been set him. Not satisfied with the force put under his command, he collected five hundred ships and one hundred and twenty thousand men. With these he swept the pirates from the seas and stormed their strongholds, and all in less than three months. Twenty thousand prisoners fell into his hands. With unusual humanity he spared their lives, and thinking that man was the creature of circumstances, determined to change their manner of life. They were to be removed from the sea, should cease to be sailors, and become farmers. It is possible that the old man of Corycus, whose skill in gardening Virgil celebrates in one of his Georgics, was one of the pirates whom the judicious mercy of Pompey changed into a useful citizen.

A still greater success remained to be won. For more than twenty years war, occasionally intercepted by periods of doubtful peace, had been carried on between Rome and Mithridates, king of Pontus. This prince, though reduced more than once to the greatest extremities, had contrived with extraordinary skill and courage to retrieve his fortunes, and now in 67 B.C. was in possession of the greater part of his original dominion. Lucullus, a general of the greatest ability, was in command of the forces of Rome, but he had lost the confidence of his troops, and affairs were at a standstill. Pompey's friends proposed that the supreme command should be transferred to him, and the law, which Cicero supported in what is perhaps the most perfect of his political speeches,[1] was passed. Pompey at once proceeded to the East. For four years Mithridates held out, but with little hope of ultimate success or even of escape. In 64, after vainly attempting to poison himself, such was the power of the antidotes by which he had fortified himself against domestic

---

[1] The Pro Lege Manilia. The law was proposed by one Manilius, a tribune of the people.

treachery (for so the story runs), he perished by
the sword of one of his mercenaries. For two
years more Pompey was busied in settling the
affairs of the East. At last, in 61, he returned
to Rome to enjoy a third triumph, and that the
most splendid which the city had ever witnessed.
It lasted for two days, but still the time was too
short for the display of the spoils of victory.
The names of no less than fifteen conquered
nations were carried in procession. A thousand
forts, nine hundred cities, had been taken, and
the chief of them were presented by means of
pictures to the eyes of the people. The revenue
of the State had been almost doubled by these
conquests. Ninety thousand talents in gold
and silver coin were paid into the treasury, nor
was this at the expense of the soldiers, whose
prize money was so large that the smallest
share amounted to fifty pounds. Never before
was such a sight seen in the world, and if
Pompey had died when it was finished, he
would have been proclaimed the most fortunate
of mankind.

Certainly he was never so great again as he
was that day. When with Cæsar and Crassus

he divided all the power of the State, he was
only the second, and by far the second, of the
three. His influence, his prestige, his popularity declined year by year. The good fortune
which had followed him without ceasing from
his earliest years now seemed to desert him.
Even the shows, the most magnificent ever
seen in the city, with which he entertained the
people at the dedication of his theater (built at
his own expense for the public benefit) were
not wholly a success. Here is a letter of
Cicero about them to his friend Marius ;
interesting as giving both a description of the
scene and as an account of the writer's own
feelings about it. " If it was some bodily pain
or weakness of health that kept you from
coming to the games, I must attribute your
absence to fortune rather than to a judicious
choice. But if you thought the things which
most men admire contemptible, and so, though
health permitted, would not come, then I am
doubly glad ; glad both that you were free from
illness and that you were so vigorous in mind
as to despise the sights which others so unreasonably admire. . . . Generally the shows were

most splendid, but not to your taste, if I may judge of yours by my own. First, the veteran actors who for their own honor had retired from the stage, returned to it to do honor to Pompey. Your favorite, my dear friend Æsopus, acquitted himself so poorly as to make us all feel that he had best retire. When he came to the oath—

' And if of purpose set I break my faith,'

his voice failed him. What need to tell you more ? You know all about the other shows ; they had not even the charm which moderate shows commonly have. The ostentation with which they were furnished forth took away all their gayety. What charm is there in having six hundred mules in the *Clytemnestra* or three thousand supernumeraries in the *Trojan Horse*, or cavalry and infantry in foreign equipment in some battle-piece. The populace admired all this ; but it would have given you no kind of pleasure. After this came a sort of wild-beast fights, lasting for five days. They were splendid : no man denies it. But what man of culture can feel any pleasure when some poor fellow is torn in pieces by some powerful animal, or when some noble animal is run through with a hunting spear. If these things are worth seeing, you have seen them before. And I, who was actually present, saw nothing new. The last day was given up to the elephants. Great was the astonishment of the crowd at the sight ; but of pleasure there was nothing. Nay, there was some feeling of compassion, some sense that this animal has a certain kinship with man." The elder Pliny tells us that two hundred lions were killed on this occasion, and that the pity felt for the elephants rose to the height of absolute rage. So lamentable was the spectacle of their despair, so pitifully did they implore the mercy of the audience, " that the whole multitude rose in tears and called down upon Pompey the curses which soon descended on him."

And then Pompey's young wife, Julia, Cæsar's daughter, died. She had been a bond of union between the two men, and the hope of peace was sensibly lessened by her loss. Perhaps the first rupture would have come any how ; when it did come it found Pompey quite unprepared for the conflict. He seemed indeed to be a match for his rival, but his strength collapsed almost at a touch. "I have but to stamp with my foot," he said on one occasion, "and soldiers will spring up;" yet when Cæsar declared war by crossing the Rubicon, he fled without a struggle. In little more than a year and a half all was over. The battle of Pharsalia was fought on the 9th of August, and on September the 29th the man who had triumphed over three continents lay a naked, headless corpse on the shore of Egypt.

CHAPTER X.

THE suppression of the "Great Conspiracy" was certainly the most glorious achievement of Cicero's life. Honors such as had never before been bestowed on a citizen of Rome were heaped upon him. Men of the highest rank spoke of him both in the Senate and before the people as the "Father of his fatherland." A public thanksgiving, such as was ordered when great victories had been won, was offered in his name. Italy was even more enthusiastic than the capital. The chief towns voted him such honors as they could bestow ; Capua in particular erected to him a gilded statue, and gave him the title of Patron of the city.

Still there were signs of trouble in the future. It was the duty of the consul on quitting office to swear that he had discharged his duty with fidelity, and it was usual for him at the same time to make a speech in which he narrated the events of his consulship. Cicero was preparing to speak when one of the new tribunes intervened. "A man," he cried, "who has put citizens to death without hearing them in their defense is not worthy to speak. He must do nothing more than take the oath." Cicero was ready with his answer. Raising his voice he said, "I swear that I, and I alone, have saved this commonwealth and this city." The assembly shouted their approval ; and when the ceremony was concluded the whole multitude escorted the ex-consul to his house. The time was not come for his enemies to attack him ; but that he had enemies was manifest.

With one dangerous man he had the misfortune to come into collision in the year that followed his consulship. This was the Clodius of whom we have heard something in the preceding chapter. The two men had hitherto been on fairly good terms. Clodius, as we have seen, belonged to one of the noblest families in Rome, was a man of some ability and wit, and could make himself agreeable when he was pleased to do so. But events for which Cicero was not in the least to blame brought about a life-long enmity between them. Toward the close of the year Clodius had been guilty of an act of scandalous impiety, intruding himself, disguised as a woman, into some peculiarly sacred rites which the matrons of Rome were accustomed to perform in honor of the " Good Goddess." He had powerful friends, and an attempt was made to screen him, which Cicero, who was genuinely indignant at the fellow's wickedness, seems to have resisted. In the end he was put upon his trial, though it was before a jury which had been specially packed for the occasion. His defense was an *alibi*, an attempt, that is, to prove that he was elsewhere on the night when he was alleged to have misconducted himself at Rome. He brought forward witnesses who swore that they had seen him at the very time at Interamna, a town in Umbria, and a place which was distant at least two days' journey from Rome. To rebut this evidence Cicero was brought forward by the prosecution. As he stepped forward the partisans of the accused set up a howl of disapproval. But the jury paid him the high compliment of rising from their seats, and the uproar ceased. He deposed that Clodius had been at his house on the morning of the day in question.

Clodius was acquitted. If evidence had any thing to do with the result, it was the conduct of Cæsar that saved him. It was in his house that the alleged intrusion had taken place, and he had satisfied himself by a private examination of its inmates that the charge was true. But now he professed to know nothing at all about the matter. Probably the really potent influence in the case was the money which Crassus liberally distributed among the jurors. The fact of the money was indeed notorious. Some of the jury had pretended that they were in fear of their lives, and had asked for a guard. "A guard!" said Catulus, to one of them, "what did you want a guard for? that the money should not be taken from you?"

But Clodius, though he had escaped, never forgave the man whose evidence had been given against him. Cicero too felt that there was war to the knife between them. On the first meeting of the Senate after the conclusion of the trial he made a pointed attack upon his old acquaintance. " Lentulus," he said, " was twice acquitted, and Catiline twice, and now this third malefactor has been let loose on the commonwealth by his judges. But, Clodius, do not misunderstand what has happened. It is for the prison, not for the city, that your judges have kept you ; not to keep you in the country, but to deprive you of the privilege of exile was what they intended. Be of good cheer, then, Fathers. No new evil has come upon us, but we have found out the evil that exists. One villain has been put upon his trial, and the result has taught us that there are more villains than one."

Clodius attempted to banter his antagonist. " You are a fine gentleman," he said ; " you have been at Baiæ " (Baiæ was a fashionable watering-place on the Campanian coast). "Well," said Cicero, " that is better than to have been at the 'matrons' worship.'" And the attack and repartee went on. " You have bought a fine house." (Cicero had spent a large sum of money on a house on the Palatine, and was known to have somewhat crippled his means by doing so.) "With you the buying has been of jurymen." "They gave you no credit though you spoke on oath." "Yes ; five-and-twenty gave me credit" (five-and-twenty of the jury had voted for a verdict of guilty ; two-and thirty for acquittal), "but your thirty-two gave you none, for they would have their money down." The Senate shouted applause, and Clodius sat down silent and confounded.

How Clodius contrived to secure for himself the office of tribune, the vantage ground from which he hoped to work his revenge, has been already told in the sketch of Cæsar. Cæsar indeed was really responsible for all that was done. It was he who made it possible for Clodius to act ; and he allowed him to act when he could have stopped him by the lifting of his finger. He was determined to prove to Cicero that he was master. But he never showed himself after the first interference in the matter of the adoption. He simply allowed Clodius to work his will without hindrance.

Clodius proceeded with considerable skill. He proposed various laws, which were so popular that Cicero, though knowing that they would be turned against himself, did not venture to oppose them. Then came a proposal directly leveled at him. " Any man who shall have put to death a Roman citizen uncondemned and without a trial is forbidden fire and water." (This was the form of a sentence of exile. No one was allowed under penalty of death to furnish the condemned with fire and water within a certain distance of Rome.) Cicero at once assumed the squalid dress with which it was the custom for accused persons to endeavor to arouse the compassion of their fellow-citizens. Twenty thousand of the upper classes supported him by their presence. The Senate itself, on the motion of one of the tribunes, went into this strange kind of mourning on his account.

The consuls of the year were Gabinus and Piso. The first was notoriously hostile, of the second Cicero hoped to make a friend, the more so as he was a kinsman of his daughter's husband. He gives a lively picture of an interview with him. " It was nearly eleven o'clock in the morning when we went to him. He came out of a dirty hovel to meet us, with his slippers on, and his head muffled up. His breath smelt most odiously of wine; but he excused himself on the score of his health, which compelled him, he said, to use medicines in which wine was employed." His answer to the petition of his visitors (for Cicero was accompanied by his son-in-law) was at least commendably frank. "My colleague Gabinius is in absolute poverty, and does not know where to turn. Without a province he must be ruined. A province he hopes to get by the help of Clodius, but it must be by my acting with him. I must humor his wishes, just as you, Cicero, humored your colleague when you were consul. But indeed there is no reason why you should seek the consul's protection. Every one must look out for himself."

In default of the consuls there was still some hope that Pompey might be induced to interfere, and Cicero sought an interview with him. Plutarch says that he slipped out by a back door to avoid seeing him; but Cicero's own account is that the interview was granted. "When I threw myself at his feet" (he means,

I suppose, humiliated himself by asking such a favor), " he could not lift me from the ground. He could do nothing, he said, against the will of Cæsar."

Cicero had now to choose between two courses. He might stay and do his best with the help of his friends, to resist the passing of the law. But this would have ended, it was well known, in something like an open battle in the streets of Rome. Clodius and his partisans were ready to carry their proposal by force of arms, and would yield to nothing but superior strength. It was possible, even probable, that in such a conflict Cicero would be victorious. But he shrank from the trial, not from cowardice, for he had courage enough when occasion demanded, not even from unwillingness to risk the lives of his friends, though this weighed somewhat with him, but chiefly because he hated to confess that freedom was becoming impossible in Rome, and that the strong hand of a master was wanted to give any kind of security to life and property. The other course was to anticipate the sentence and to go into voluntary exile. This was the course which his most powerful friends pressed upon him, and this was the course which he chose. He left Rome, intending to go to Sicily, where he knew that he should find the heartiest of welcomes.

Immediately on his departure Clodius formally proposed his banishment. " Let it be enacted," so ran the proposition, " that, seeing that Marcus Tullius Cicero has put Roman citizens to death without trial, forging thereto the authority of the Senate, that he be forbidden fire and water ; that no one harbor or receive him on pain of death ; and that whosoever shall move, shall vote, or take any steps for the recalling of him, be dealt with as a public enemy." The bill was passed, the distance within which it was to operate being fixed at four hundred miles. The houses of the banished man were razed to the ground, the site of the mansion on the Palatine being dedicated to Liberty. His property was partly plundered, partly sold by auction.

Cicero meanwhile had hurried to the south of Italy. He found shelter for a while at the farm of a friend near Vibo in Brutii (now the

Abruzzi), but found it necessary to leave this place because it was within the prescribed limits. Sicily was forbidden to him by its governor, who, though a personal friend, was unwilling to displease the party in power. Athens, which for many reasons he would have liked to choose for his place of exile, was unsafe. He had bitter enemies there, men who had been mixed up in Catiline's conspiracy. The place, too, was within the distance, and though this was not very strictly insisted upon—as a matter of fact, he did spend the greater part of his banishment inside the prescribed limit—it might at any moment be made a means of annoyance. Atticus invited him to take up his residence at his seat at Buthrotum in Epirus (now Albania). But the proposal did not commend itself to his taste. It was out of the way, and would be very dreary without the presence of its master, who was still at Rome, and apparently intended to remain there. After staying for about a fort-night at a friend's house near Dyrrachium— the town itself, where he was once very popu-lar, for fear of bringing some trouble upon it, he refused to enter—he crossed over to Greece, and ultimately settled himself at Thessalonica.

Long afterward he tells us of a singular dream which seems to have given him some little comfort at this time. " I had lain awake for the greater part of the night, but fell into a heavy slumber toward morning. I was at the point of starting, but my host would not allow me to be waked. At seven o'clock, however, I rose, and then told my friend this dream. I seemed to myself to be wandering disconsolately in some lonely place when the great Marius met me. His lictors were with him, their *fasces* wreathed with bays. ' Why are you so sad?' he asked me. 'I have been wrongly banished from my country,' I answered. He then took my hand, and turning to the nearest lictor, bade him lead me to his own Memorial Hall. ' There,' he said, 'you will be safe.'" His friend declared that this dream portended a speedy and honorable return. Curiously enough it was in the Hall of Marius that the decree repealing the sentence of banishment was actually proposed and passed.

For the most part he was miserably unhappy

and depressed. In letter after letter he poured out to Atticus his fears, his complaints, and his wants. Why had he listened to the bad advice of his friends? He had wished to stay at Rome and fight out the quarrel. Why had Hortensius advised him to retire from the struggle? It must have been jealousy, jealousy of one whom he knew to be a more successful advocate than himself. Why had Atticus hindered his purposes when he thought of putting an end to all his trouble by killing himself? Why were all his friends, why was Atticus himself, so lukewarm in his cause? In one letter he artfully reproaches himself for his neglect of his friends in times past as the cause of their present indifference. But the reproach is of course really leveled at them.

"If ever," he writes in one letter, "fortune shall restore me to my country and to you, I will certainly take care that of all my friends none shall be more rejoiced than you. All my duty to you, a duty which I must own in time past was sadly wanting, shall be so faithfully discharged that you will feel that I have been restored to you quite as much as I shall have been restored to my brother and to my children. For whatever I have wronged you, and indeed because I have wronged you, pardon me; for I have wronged myself far worse. I do not write this as not knowing that you feel the very greatest trouble on my account; but if you were and had been under the obligation to love me, as much as you actually do love me and have loved me, you never would have allowed me to lack the wise advice which you have so abundantly at your command." This is perhaps a little obscure, as it is certainly somewhat subtle; but Cicero means that Atticus had not interested himself in his affairs as much as he would have felt bound to do, if he (Cicero) had been less remiss in the duties of friendship.

To another correspondent, his wife Terentia, he poured out his heart yet more freely. " Don't think," he writes in one of his letters to her, " that I write longer letters to others than to you, except indeed I have received some long communication which I feel I must answer. Indeed I have nothing to write; and in these days I find it the most difficult of duties.

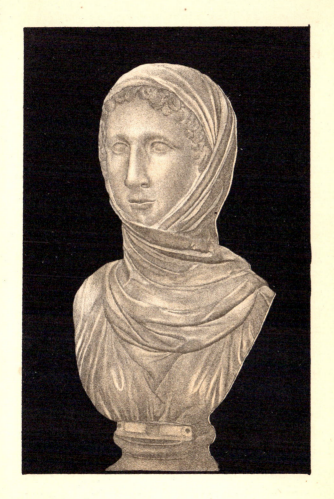

A Vestal Virgin.

Writing to you and to my dearest Tullia I never can do without floods of tears. I see you are utterly miserable, and I wanted you to be completely happy. I might have made you so. I could have made you had I been less timid . . . . My heart's delight, my deepest regret is to think that you, to whom all used to look for help, should now be involved in such sorrow, such distress! and that I should be to blame, I who saved others only to ruin myself and mine! . . . . As for expenditure, let others, who can if they will, undertake it. And if you love me, don't distress your health, which is already, I know, feeble. All night, all day I think of you. I see that you are undertaking all imaginable labors on my behalf; I only fear that you will not be able to endure them. I am aware that all depends upon you. If we are to succeed in what you wish and are now trying to compass, take care of your health." In another he writes: "Unhappy that I am! to think that one so virtuous, so loyal, so honest, so kind, should be so afflicted, and all on my account. And my dearest Tullia, too, that she should be so unhappy about a father in whom she once found so much happiness. And what shall I say about my dear little Cicero? That he should feel the bitterest sorrow and trouble as soon as he began to feel any thing! If all this was really, as you write, the work of fate, I could endure it a little more easily ; but it was all brought about by my fault, thinking that I was loved by men who really were jealous of me, and keeping aloof from others who were really on my side."

This is, perhaps, a good opportunity of saying something about the lady herself. Who she was we do not certainly know. There was a family of the name in Rome, the most notable of whom perhaps was the Terentius Varro [1] whose rashness brought upon his country the terrible disaster of the defeat of Cannæ. She had a half-sister, probably older than herself, of the name of Fabia, who was a vestal virgin. She brought her husband, to whom she was married about 78 B.C., a fair dowry, about three thousand five hundred pounds. We have seen how affectionately Cicero writes to her during

[1] Another of the same name was an eminent man of letters of Cicero's own time.

his exile. She is his darling, his only hope ;
the mere thought of her makes his eyes over-
flow with tears. And she seems to have deserved all his praise and affection, exerting
herself to the utmost to help him, and ready to
impoverish herself to find him the means that he
needed. Four letters of this period have been
preserved. There are twenty others belonging
to the years 50–47 B.C. The earlier of these
are sufficiently affectionate. When he is about
to return to Rome from his province (Cilicia),
she is still the most amiable, the dearest of
women. Then we begin to see signs of coolness, yet nothing that would strike us did we
not know what was afterwards to happen. He
excuses the rarity of his letters. There is no
one by whom to send them. If there were, he
was willing to write. The greetings became
formal, the superlatives " dearest," " fondest,"
" best," are dropped. " You are glad," he writes
after the battle of Pharsalia had dashed his
hopes, " that I have got back safe to Italy ; I
hope that you may continue to be glad."
" Don't think of coming," he goes on, " it is a
long journey and not very safe ; and I don't see

what good you would do if you should come."
In another letter he gives directions about
getting ready his house at Tusculum for the
reception of guests. The letter is dated on
the first of October, and he and his friends
would come probably to stay several days, on
the seventh. If there was not a tub in the
bath-room, one must be provided. The greeting is of the briefest and most formal. Meanwhile we know from what he writes to Atticus
that he was greatly dissatisfied with the lady's
conduct. Money matters were at the bottom
of their quarrel. She was careless, he thinks,
and extravagant. Though he was a rich man,
yet he was often in need of ready money, and
Terentia could not be relied upon to help him.
His vexation takes form in a letter to Atticus.
"As to Terentia—there are other things without number of which I don't speak—what
can be worse than this? You wrote to her
to send me bills for one hundred and eight
pounds ; for there was so much money left
in hand. She sent me just ninety pounds,
and added a note that this was all. If she was
capable of abstracting such a trifle from so small

a sum, don't you see what she would have done in matters of real importance?" The quarrel ended in a divorce, a thing far more common than, happily, it is among ourselves, but still a painful and discreditable end to an union which had lasted for more than five-and-twenty years. Terentia long survived her husband, dying in extreme old age (as much, it was said, as a hundred and three years), far on in the reign of Augustus; and after a considerable experience of matrimony, if it be true that she married three or even, according to some acounts, four other husbands.

Terentia's daughter, Tullia, had a short and unhappy life. She was born, it would seem, about 79 B.C., and married when fifteen or sixteen to a young Roman noble, Piso Frugi by name. " The best, the most loyal of men," Cicero calls him. He died in 57 B.C., and Rome lost, if his father-in-law's praises of him may be trusted, an orator of the very highest promise. " I never knew any one who surpassed my son-in-law, Piso, in zeal, in industry, and, I may fairly say, in ability." The next year she married a certain Crassipes, a very shadowy person indeed. We know nothing of what manner of man he was, or what became of him. But in 50 B.C. Tullia was free to marry again. Her third venture was of her own or her mother's contriving. Her father was at his government in Cilicia, and he hears of the affair with surprise. " Believe me," he writes to Atticus, "nothing could have been less expected by me. Tiberius Nero had made proposals to me, and I had sent friends to discuss the matter with the ladies. But when they got to Rome the betrothal had taken place. This, I hope, will be a better match. I fancy the ladies were very much pleased with the young gentleman's complaisance and cour- tesy, but do not look for the thorns." The " thorns," however, were there. A friend who kept Cicero acquainted with the news of Rome, told him as much, though he wraps up his meaning in the usual polite phrases. " I con- gratulate you," he writes, " on your alliance with one who is, I really believe, a worthy fellow. I do indeed think this of him. If there have been some things in which he has not done justice to himself, these are now past

and gone ; any traces that may be left will soon,
I am sure, disappear, thanks to your good influence and to his respect for Tullia. He is
not offensive in his errors, and does not seem
slow to appreciate better things." Tullia, however, was not more successful than other wives
in reforming her husband. Her marriage
seems to have been unhappy almost from the
beginning. It was brought to an end by a
divorce after about three years. Shortly afterward Tullia, who could have been little more
than thirty, died, to the inconsolable grief of
her father. " My grief," he writes to Atticus,
" passes all consolation. Yet I have done what
certainly no one ever did before, written a
treatise for my own consolation. (I will send
you the book if the copyists have finished it.)
And indeed there is nothing like it. I write
day after day, and all day long ; not that I can
get any good from it, but it occupies me a
little, not much indeed ; the violence of my
grief is too much for me. Still I am soothed,
and do my best to compose, not my feelings,
indeed, but, if I can, my face." And again :
" Next to your company nothing is more agree-

able to me than solitude. Then all my converse is with books ; yet this is interrupted by tears; these I resist as well as I can ; but at present I fail." At one time he thought of finding comfort in unusual honors to the dead. He would build a shrine of which Tullia should be the deity. " I am determined," he writes, "on building the shrine. From this purpose I cannot be turned . . . . Unless the building be finished this summer, I shall hold myself guilty." He fixes upon a design. He begs Atticus, in one of his letters, to buy some columns of marble of Chios for the building. He discusses the question of the site. Some gardens near Rome strike him as a convenient place. It must be conveniently near if it is to attract worshipers. " I would sooner sell or mortgage, or live on little, than be disappointed." Then he thought that he would build it on the grounds of his villa. In the end he did not build it at all. Perhaps the best memorial of Tullia is the beautiful letter in which one of Cicero's friends seeks to console him for his loss. " She had lived," he says, " as long as life was worth living, as long

as the republic stood." One passage, though
it has often been quoted before, I must give.
" I wish to tell you of something which brought
me no small consolation, hoping that it may
also somewhat diminish your sorrow. On my
way back from Asia, as I was sailing from
Ægina to Megara, I began to contemplate the
places that lay around me. Behind me was
Ægina, before me Megara; on my right hand
the Piræus, on my left hand Corinth; towns
all of them that were once at the very height
of prosperity, but now lie ruined and desolate
before our eyes. I began thus to reflect:
'Strange! do we, poor creatures of a day, bear
it ill if one of us perish of disease, or are
slain with the sword, we whose life is bound
to be short, while the dead bodies of so many
lie here inclosed within so small a compass?'"

But I am anticipating. When Cicero was in
exile the republic had yet some years to live;
and there were hopes that it might survive altogether. The exile's prospects, too, began to
brighten. Cæsar had reached for the present
the height of his ambition, and was busy with
his province of Gaul. Pompey had quarreled

with Clodius, whom he found to be utterly unmanageable. And Cicero's friend, one Milo, of whom I shall have to say more hereafter, being the most active of them all, never ceased to agitate for his recall. It would be tedious to recall all the vicissitudes of the struggle. As early as May the Senate passed a resolution repealing the decree of banishment, the news of it having caused an outburst of joy in the city. Accius' drama of "Telamon" was being acted at the time, and the audience applauded each senator as he entered the Senate, and rose from their places to greet the consul as he came in. But the enthusiasm rose to its height when the actor who was playing the part of Telamon (whose banishment from his country formed part of the action of the drama) declaimed with significant emphasis the following lines—

> What! he—the man who still with steadfast heart
> Strove for his country, who in perilous days
> Spared neither life nor fortune, and bestowed
> Most help when most she needed; who surpassed
> In wit all other men.   Father of Gods,
> *His* house—yea, *his !*—I saw devoured by fire ;
> And ye, ungrateful, foolish, without thought
> Of all wherein he served you, could endure

> To see him banished ; yea, and to this hour
> Suffer that he prolong an exile's day.

Still obstacle after obstacle was interposed, and it was not till the fourth of August that the decree passed through all its stages and became finally law. Cicero, who had been waiting at the point of Greece nearest to Italy, to take the earliest opportunity of returning, had been informed by his friends that he might now safely embark. He sailed accordingly on the very day when the decree was passed, and reached Brundisium on the morrow. It happened to be the day on which the foundation of the colony was celebrated, and also the birthday of Tullia, who had come so far to meet her father. The coincidence was observed by the townspeople with delight. On the eighth the welcome news came from Rome, and Cicero set out for the capital. "All along my road the cities of Italy kept the day of my arrival as a holiday; the ways were crowded with the deputations which were sent from all parts to congratulate me. When I approached the city, my coming was honored by such a concourse of men, such a heartiness of congratulation as are past believing. The way from the gates, the ascent of the Capitol, the return to my home made such a spectacle that in the very height of my joy I could not but be sorry that a people so grateful had yet been so unhappy, so cruelly oppressed." "That day," he said emphatically, "that day was as good as immortality to me."

CHAPTER XI.

A BRAWL AND ITS CONSEQUENCES.

CLODIUS, who had taken the lead in driving Cicero into exile, was of course furious at his return, and continued to show him an unceasing hostility. His first care was to hinder the restoration of his property. He had contrived to involve part at least of this in a considerable difficulty. Cicero's house on the Palatine Hill had been pulled down and the area dedicated —so at least Clodius alleged—to the Goddess of Liberty. If this was true, it was sacred forever ; it could not be restored. The question was, Was it true ? This question was referred to the Pontiffs as judges of such matters. Cicero argued the case before them, and they pronounced in his favor. It was now for the Senate to act. A motion was made that the site should be restored. Clodius opposed it, talking for three hours, till the anger of his audience compelled him to bring his speech to an end. One of the tribunes in his interest put his veto on the motion, but was frightened into withdrawing it. But Clodius was not at the end of his resources. A set of armed ruffians under his command drove out the workmen who were rebuilding the house. A few days afterwards he made an attack on Cicero himself. He was wounded in the struggle which followed, and might, says Cicero, have been killed, "but," he adds, "I am tired of surgery."

Pompey was another object of his hatred, for he knew perfectly well that without his consent his great enemy would not have been restored. Cicero gives a lively picture of a scene in the Senate, in which this hatred was vigorously expressed. "Pompey spoke, or rather wished to speak; for, as soon as he rose, Clodius' hired ruffians shouted at him. All through his speech it was the same; he was interrupted not only by shouts but by abuse and curses. When he came to an end—and it must be allowed that he showed courage; nothing frightened him: he said his say and sometimes even obtained silence—then Clodius rose. He was met with such an uproar from our side (for we had determined to give him back as good as he had given) that he could not collect his thoughts, control his speech, or command his countenance. This went on from three o'clock, when Pompey had only just finished his speech, till five. Meanwhile every kind of abuse, even to ribald verses, were shouted out against Clodius and his sister. Pale with fury he turned to his followers, and in the midst of the uproar asked them, 'Who is it that is killing the people with hunger?' 'Pompey,' they answered. 'Who wants to go to Alexandria?' 'Pompey,' they answered again. 'And whom do *you* want to go?' 'Crassus,' they said. About six o'clock the party of Clodius began, at some given signal, it seemed, to spit at our side. Our rage now burst out. They tried to drive us from our place, and we made a charge. The partisans of Clodius fled. He was thrust down from the hustings. I then made my escape, lest any thing worse should happen."

A third enemy, and one whom Clodius was

destined to find more dangerous than either Cicero or Pompey, was Annius Milo. Milo was on the mother's side of an old Latin family. The name by which he was commonly known was probably a nickname given him, it may be, in joking allusion to the Milo of Crotona, the famous wrestler, who carried an ox on his shoulders and ate it in a single day. For Milo was a great fighting man, a well-born gladiator, one who was for cutting all political knots with the sword. He was ambitious, and aspired to the consulship; but the dignity was scarcely within his reach. His family was not of the highest; he was deeply in debt; he had neither eloquence nor ability. His best chance, therefore, was to attach himself to some powerful friend whose gratitude he might earn. Just such a friend he seemed to find in Cicero. He saw the great orator's fortunes were very low, but they would probably rise again, and he would be grateful to those who helped him in his adversity. Hence Milo's exertions to bring him back from banishment and hence the quarrel with Clodius. The two men had their bands of hired, or rather purchased, ruffians about the city, and came into frequent collisions. Each indicted the other for murderous assault. Each publicly declared that he should take the earliest chance of putting his enemy to death. What was probably a chance collision brought matters to a crisis.

On the twentieth of January Milo left Rome to pay a visit to Lanuvium, a Latin town on the Appian road, and about fifteen miles south of Rome. It was a small town, much decayed from the old days when its revolt against Rome was thought to be a thing worth recording ; but it contained one of the most famous temples of Italy, the dwelling of Juno the Preserver, whose image, in its goat-skin robe, its quaint, turned-up shoes, with spear in one hand and small shield in the other, had a peculiar sacredness. Milo was a native of the place, and its dictator; and it was his duty on this occasion to nominate the chief priest of the temple. He had been at a meeting of the Senate in the morning, and had remained till the close of the sitting. Returning home he had changed his dress and shoes, waited a while, as men have to wait, says Cicero, while his wife was getting ready, and then started. He traveled in a carriage with his wife and a friend. Several maid-servants and a troop of singing boys belonging to his wife followed. Much was made of this great retinue of women and boys, as proving that Milo had no intention when he started of coming to blows with his great enemy. But he had also with him a number of armed slaves and several gladiators, among whom were two famous masters of their art. He had traveled about ten miles when he met Clodius, who had been delivering an address to the town council of Aricia, another Latin town, nearer to the capital than Lanuvium, and was now returning to Rome. He was on horseback, contrary to his usual custom, which was to use a carriage, and he had with him thirty slaves armed with swords. No person of distinction thought of traveling without such attendants.

The two men passed each other, but Milo's gladiators fell out with the slaves of Clodius. Clodius rode back and accosted the aggressors in a threatening manner. One of the gladiators replied by wounding him in the shoulder with his sword. A number of Milo's slaves hastened back to assist their comrades. The party of Clodius was overpowered, and Clodius himself, exhausted by his wound, took refuge in a roadside tavern, which probably marked the first stage out of Rome. Milo, thinking that now he had gone so far he might go a little further and rid himself of his enemy forever, ordered his slaves to drag Clodius from his refuge and finish him. This was promptly done. Cicero indeed declared that the slaves did it without orders, and in the belief that their master had been killed. But Rome believed the other story. The corpse of the dead man lay for some time upon the road uncared for, for all his attendants had either fallen in the struggle or had crept into hiding-places. Then a Roman gentleman on his way to the city ordered it to be put into his litter and taken to Rome, where it arrived just before nightfall. It was laid out in state in the hall of his mansion, and his widow stood by showing the wounds to the sympathizing crowd which thronged to see his remains. Next day the excitement increased. Two of the tribunes suggested that the body should be carried into the market-place, and placed on the hustings from which the speaker commonly addressed the people. Then it was resolved, at the suggestion of another Clodius, a notary, and a client of the family, to do it a signal honor. "Thou shalt not bury or burn a man within the city" was one of the oldest of Roman laws. Clodius, the favorite of the people, should be an exception. His body was carried into the Hall of Hostilius, the usual meeting-place of the Senate. The benches, the tables, the platform from which the orators spoke, the wooden tablets on which the clerks wrote their notes, were collected to make a funeral pile on which the corpse was to be consumed. The hall caught fire, and was burned to the ground; another large building adjoining it, the Hall of Porcius, narrowly escaped the same fate. The mob attacked several houses, that of Milo among them, and was with difficulty repulsed.

It had been expected that Milo would voluntarily go into exile; but the burning of the senate-house caused a strong reaction of feeling of which he took advantage. He re-

turned to Rome, and provided to canvass for
the consulship, making a present in money
(which may be reckoned at five-and-twenty
shillings) to every voter. The city was in a
continual uproar ; though the time for the new
consuls to enter on their office was long past,
they had not even been elected, nor was there
any prospect, such was the violence of the
rival candidates, of their being so. At last the
Senate had recourse to the only man who
seemed able to deal with the situation, and
appointed Pompey sole consul. Pompey proposed to institute for the trial of Milo's case
a special court with a special form of pro-
cedure. The limits of the time which it was
to occupy were strictly laid down. Three
days were to be given to the examination of
witnesses, one to the speeches of counsel, the
prosecution being allowed two hours only, the
defense three. After a vain resistance on the
part of Milo's friends, the proposal was carried,
Pompey threatening to use force if necessary.
Popular feeling now set very strongly against
the accused. Pompey proclaimed that he went
in fear of his life from his violence ; refused to

appear in the Senate lest he should be assassinated, and even left his house to live in his gardens, which could be more effectually guarded by soldiers. In the Senate Milo was accused of having arms under his clothing, a charge which he had to disprove by lifting up his under garment. Next a freedman came forward, and declared that he and four others had actually seen the murder of Clodius, and that having mentioned the fact, they had been seized and shut up for two months in Milo's counting-house. Finally a sheriff's officer, if we may so call him, deposed that another important witness, one of Milo's slaves, had been forcibly taken out of his hands by the partisans of the accused.

On the eighth of April the trial was begun. The first witness called was a friend who had been with Clodius on the day of his death. His evidence made the case look very dark against Milo, and the counsel who was to cross-examine him on behalf of the accused was received with such angry cries that he had to take refuge on the bench with the presiding judge. Milo was obliged to ask for the same protection.

Pompey resolved that better order should be kept for the future, and occupied all the approaches to the court with troops. The rest of the witnesses were heard and cross-examined without interruption. April 11th was the last day of the trial. Three speeches were delivered for the prosecution ; for the defense one only, and that by Cicero. It had been suggested that he should take the bold line of arguing that Clodius was a traitor, and that the citizen who slew him had deserved well of his country. But he judged it better to follow another course, and to show that Clodius had been the aggressor, having deliberately laid an ambush for Milo, of whose meditated journey to Lanuvium he was of course aware. Unfortunately for his client the case broke down. Milo had evidently left Rome and the conflict had happened much earlier than was said, because the body of the murdered man had reached the capital not later than five o'clock in the afternoon. This disproved the assertion that Clodius had loitered on his way back to Rome till the growing darkness gave him an opportunity of attacking his adversaries. Then it came out that

Milo had had in his retinue, besides the women and boys, a number of fighting men. Finally there was the damning fact, established, it would seem, by competent witnesses, that Clodius had been dragged from his hiding-place and put to death. Cicero too lost his presence of mind. The sight of the city, in which all the shops were shut in expectation of a riot, the presence of the soldiers in court, and the clamor of a mob furiously hostile to the accused and his advocate, confounded him, and he spoke feebly and hesitatingly. The admirable oration which has come down to us, and professes to have been delivered on this occasion, was really written afterwards. The jury, which was allowed by common consent to have been one of the best ever assembled, gave a verdict of guilty. Milo went into banishment at Marseilles—a punishment which he seems to have borne very easily, if it is true that when Cicero excused himself for the want of courage which had marred the effect of his defense, he answered, "It was all for the best ; if you had spoken better I should never have tasted these admirable Marseilles mullets."

Naturally he tired of the mullets before long. When Cæsar had made himself master of Rome, he hoped to be recalled from banishment. But Cæsar did not want him, and preferred to have him where he was. Enraged at this treatment, he came over to Italy and attempted to raise an insurrection in favor of Pompey. The troops whom he endeavored to corrupt refused to follow him. He retreated with his few followers into the extreme south of the peninsula, and was there killed.

CHAPTER XII.

CATO, BRUTUS, AND PORCIA.

" From his earliest years," so runs the character that has come down to us of Cato, " he
was resolute to obstinacy. Flattery met with
a rough repulse, and threats with resistance.
He never laughed, and his smile was of the
slightest. Not easily provoked, his anger, once
roused, was implacable. He learned but slowly,
but never forgot a thing once acquired ; he was
obedient to his teachers, but wanted to know
the reason of every thing." The stories told of
his boyhood bear out this character. Here is
one of them. His tutor took him to Sulla's
house. It was in the evil days of the Proscription, and there were signs of the bloody work
that was going on. " Why does no one kill this
man ?" he asked his teacher. " Because, my

son, they fear him more than they hate him,"
was the answer. " Why then," was the re-
joinder, " have you not given me a sword that
I may set my country free ? " The tutor, as it
may be supposed, carried him off in haste.

Like most young Romans he began life as a
soldier, and won golden opinions not only by
his courage, which indeed was common enough
in a nation that conquered the world, but by his
temperance and diligent performance of duty.
His time of service ended, he set out on his
travels, accepting an invitation from the tributary king of Galatia, who happened to be an
old friend of the family, to visit him. We get
an interesting little picture of a Roman of the
upper class on a tour. " At dawn he would
send on a baker and a cook to the place which
he intended to visit. These would enter the
town in a most unpretending fashion, and if
their master did not happen to have a friend or
acquaintance in the place, would betake themselves to an inn, and there prepare for their
master's accommodation without troubling any
one. It was only when there was no inn that
they went to the magistrates and asked for

entertainment ; and they were always content with what was assigned. Often they met with but scanty welcome and attention, not enforcing their demands with the customary threats, so that Cato on his arrival found nothing prepared. Nor did their master create a more favorable impression, sitting as he did quietly on his luggage, and seeming to accept the situation. Sometimes, however, he would send for the town authorities and say, " You had best give up these mean ways, my inhospitable friends ; you won't find that all your visitors are Catos." Once at least he found himself, as he thought, magnificently received. Approaching Antioch, he found the road lined on either side with troops of spectators. The men stood in one company, the boys in another. Every body was in holiday dress. Some—these were the magistrates and priests—wore white robes and garlands of flowers. Cato, supposing that all these preparations were intended for himself, was annoyed that his servants had not prevented them. But he was soon undeceived. An old man ran out from the crowd, and without so much as greeting the new comer, cried,

PORCIA, AND MARCUS PORCIUS CATO.

"Where did you leave Demetrius? When will he come?" Demetrius was Pompey's freedman, and had some of his master's greatness reflected on him. Cato could only turn away muttering, "Wretched place!"

Returning to Rome he went through the usual course of honors, always discharging his duties with the utmost zeal and integrity, and probably, as long as he filled a subordinate place, with great success. It was when statesmanship was wanted that he began to fail.

In the affair of the conspiracy of Catiline Cato stood firmly by Cicero, supporting the proposition to put the conspirators to death in a powerful speech, the only speech of all that he made that was preserved. This preservation was due to the forethought of Cicero, who put the fastest writers whom he could find to relieve each other in taking down the oration. This, it is interesting to be told, was the beginning of shorthand.

Cato, like Cicero, loved and believed in the republic ; but he was much more uncompromising, more honest perhaps we may say, but certainly less discreet in putting his principles into action. He set himself to oppose the accumulation of power in the hands of Pompey and Cæsar; but he lacked both dignity and prudence, and he accomplished nothing. When, for instance, Cæsar, returning from Spain, petitioned the Senate for permission to become a candidate for the consulship without entering the city—to enter the city would have been to abandon his hopes of a triumph—Cato condescended to use the arts of obstruction in opposing him. He spoke till sunset against the proposition, and it failed by sheer lapse of time. Yet the opposition was fruitless. Cæsar of course abandoned the empty honor, and secured the reality, all the more certainly because people felt that he had been hardly used. And so he continued to act, always seeking to do right, but always choosing the very worst way of doing it; anxious to serve his country, but always contriving to injure it. Even in that which, we may say, best became him in his life, in the leaving of it (if we accept for the moment the Roman view of the morality of suicide), he was not doing his best for Rome. Had he been willing to live (for Cæsar was ready to spare him, as he was always ready to spare enemies who could not harm him), there was yet good for him to do ; in his hasty impatience of what he disapproved, he preferred to deprive his country of its most honest citizen.

We must not omit a picture so characteristic of Roman life as the story of his last hours. The last army of the republic had been destroyed at Thapsus, and Cæsar was undisputed master of the world. Cato vainly endeavored to stir up the people of Utica, a town near Carthage, in which he had taken up his quarters; when they refused, he resolved to put an end to his life. A kinsman of Cæsar, who was preparing to intercede with the conqueror for the lives of the vanquished leaders, begged Cato's help in revising his speech. " For you," he said, " I should think it no shame to clasp his hands and fall at his knees." " Were I willing to take my life at his hands," replied Cato, " I should go alone to ask it. But I refuse to live by the favor of a tyrant. Still, as there are three hundred others for whom you are to intercede, let us see what can be done with the speech." This business finished, he took an affectionate leave of his friend, commending to his good offices his son and his friends. On his son he laid a strict injunction not to meddle with public life. Such a part as was worthy of the name of Cato no man could take again ; to take any other would be shameful. Then followed the bath, and after the bath, dinner, to which he had invited a number of friends, magistrates of the town. He sat at the meal, instead of reclining. This had been his custom ever since the fated day of Pharsalia. After dinner, over the wine, there was much learned talk, and this not other than cheerful in tone. But when the conversation happened to turn on one of the favorite maxims of the Stoics, " Only the good man is free ; the bad are slaves," Cato expressed himself with an energy and even a fierceness that made the company suspect some terrible resolve. The melancholy silence that ensued warned the speaker that he had betrayed himself, and he hastened to remove the suspicion by talking on other topics. After dinner he took his customary walk, gave the necessary orders to the officers on guard, and then sought his chamber. Here he took up the Phædo, the famous dialogue in which Socrates, on the day when he is to drink the poison, discusses the immortality of the soul. He had almost finished the book, when, chancing to turn his eyes upwards, he perceived that his sword had been removed. His son had removed it while he sat at dinner. He called a slave and asked, " Who has taken my sword ? " As the man said nothing, he resumed his book ; but in the course of a few minutes, finding that search was not being made, he asked for the sword again. Another interval followed ; and still it was not forthcoming. His anger was now roused. He vehemently reproached the slaves, and even struck one of them with his fist, which he injured by the blow. " My son and my slaves," he said, " are betraying me to the enemy." He would listen to no entreaties, "Am I a madman," he said, " that I am stripped of my arms ? Are you going to bind my hands and give me up to Cæsar ? As for the sword I can do without it ; I need but hold my breath or dash my head against the wall. It is idle to think that you can keep a man of my years alive against his will." It was felt to be impossible to persist in the face of this determination, and a young slave-boy brought back the sword. Cato felt the weapon, and finding that the blade was straight and the edge perfect, said, "Now I am my own master." He then read the Phædo again from beginning to end, and afterwards fell into so profound a sleep that persons standing outside the chamber heard his breathing. About midnight he sent for his physician and one of his freed-men. The freedman was commissioned to inquire whether his friends had set sail. The physician he asked to bind up his wounded hand, a request which his attendants heard with delight, as it seemed to indicate a resolve to live. He again sent to inquire about his friends and expressed his regret at the rough weather which they seemed likely to have. The birds were now beginning to twitter at the approach of dawn, and he fell into a short sleep. The freedman now returned with news that the harbor was quiet. When he found himself again alone, he stabbed himself with the sword, but the blow, dealt as it was by the wounded hand, was not fatal. He fell fainting on the

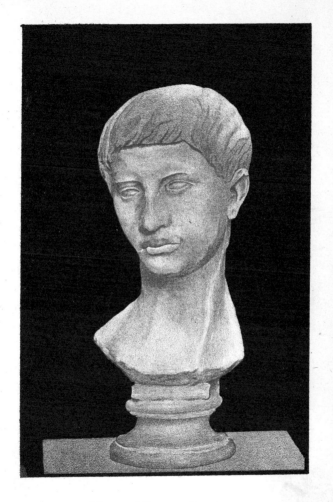

MARCUS JUNIUS BRUTUS.

couch, knocking down a counting board which stood near, and groaning. His son with others rushed into the chamber, and the physician, finding that the wound was not mortal, proceeded to bind it up. Cato, recovering his consciousness, thrust the attendants aside, and tearing open the wound, expired.

If the end of Cato's life was its noblest part, it is still more true that the fame of Brutus rests on one memorable deed. He was known, indeed, as a young man of promise, with whose education special pains had been taken, and who had a genuine love for letters and learning. He was free, it would seem, from some of the vices of his age, but he had serious faults. Indeed the one transaction of his earlier life with which we happen to be well acquainted is very little to his credit. And this, again, is so characteristic of one side of Roman life that it should be told in some detail.

Brutus had married the daughter of a certain Appius Claudius, a kinsman of the notorious Clodius, and had accompanied his father-in-law to his province, Cilicia. He took the opportunity of increasing his means by lending money to the provincials. Lending money, it must be remembered, was not thought a discreditable occupation even for the very noblest. To lend money upon interest was, indeed, the only way of making an investment, besides the buying of land, that was available to the Roman capitalist. But Brutus was more than a money-lender, he was an usurer; that is, he sought to extract an extravagantly high rate of interest from his debtors. And this greed brought him into collision with Cicero.

A certain Scaptius had been agent for Brutus in lending money to the town of Salamis in Cyprus. Under the government of Claudius, Scaptius had had every thing his own way. He had been appointed to a command in the town, had some cavalry at his disposal, and extorted from the inhabitants what terms he pleased, shutting up, it is told us, the Senate in their council-room till five of them perished of hunger. Cicero heard of this monstrous deed as he was on his way to his province; he peremptorily refused the request of Scaptius for a renewal of his command, saying that he had resolved not to grant such posts to any person engaged in trading or money-lending. Still, for Brutus' sake—and it was not for some time that it came out that Brutus was the principal—he would take care that the money should be paid. This the town was ready to do ; but then came in the question of interest. An edict had been published that this should never exceed twelve per cent., or one per cent. monthly, that being the customary way of payment. But Scaptius pleaded his bond, which provided for four per cent. monthly, and pleaded also a special edict that regulations restraining interest were not to apply to Salamis. The town protested that they could not pay if such terms were exacted —terms which would double the principal. They could not, they said, have met even the smaller claim, if it had not been for the liber- ality of the governor, who had declined the customary presents. Brutus was much vexed.

"Even when he asks me a favor," writes Cicero to Atticus, "there is always something arrogant and churlish : still he moves laughter more than anger."

When the civil war broke out between Cæsar and Pompey, it was expected that

Brutus would attach himself to the former. Pompey, who had put his father to death, he had no reason to love. But if he was unscrupulous in some things, in politics he had principles which he would not abandon, the strongest of these, perhaps, being that the side of which Cato approved was the side of the right. Pompey received his new adherent with astonishment and delight, rising from his chair to greet him. He spent most of his time in camp in study, being ingrossed on the very eve of the battle in making an epitome of Polybius, the Greek historian of the Second Punic War. He passed through the disastrous day of Pharsalia unhurt, Cæsar having given special orders that his life was to be spared. After the battle, the conqueror not only pardoned him but treated him with the greatest kindness, a kindness for which, for a time at least, he seems not to have been ungrateful. But there were influences at work which he could not resist. There was his friendship with Cassius, who had a passionate hatred against usurpers, the remembrance of how Cato had died sooner than submit himself to Cæsar, and, not least, the association of his name, which he was not permitted to forget. The statue of the old patriot who had driven out the Tarquins was covered with such in- scriptions as, " Brutus, would thou wert alive !" and Brutus' own chair of office—he was prætor at the time—was found covered with papers on which were scribbled, " Brutus, thou sleepest," or, "A true Brutus art thou," and the like. How he slew Cæsar I have told already ; how he killed himself in despair after the second battle of Philippi may be read elsewhere.

Porcia, the daughter of Cato, was left a widow in 48 B.C., and married three years afterwards her cousin Brutus, who divorced his first wife Claudia in order to marry her. She inherited both the literary tastes and the opinions of her father, and she thought herself aggrieved when her husband seemed unwilling to confide his plans to her. Plutarch thus tells her story, his authority seeming to be a little biography which one of her sons by her first husband afterwards wrote of his stepfather. " She wounded herself in the thigh with a knife such as barbers use for cutting the nails. The wound was deep, the loss of blood great, and the pain and fever that followed acute. Her husband was in the greatest distress, when his wife thus addressed him : ' Brutus, it was a daughter of Cato who became your wife, not merely to share your bed and board, but to be the partner of your adversity and your prosperity. *You* give me no cause to complain, but what proof can I give you of my affection if I may not bear with you your secret troubles. Women, I know, are weak creatures, ill fitted to keep secrets. Yet a good training and honest company may do much, and this, as Cato's daughter and wife to Brutus, I have had.' She then showed him the wound, and told him that she had inflicted it upon herself to prove her courage and constancy." For all this resolution she had something of a woman's weakness. When her husband had left the house on the day fixed for the assassination, she could not conceal her agitation. She eagerly inquired of all who entered how Brutus fared, and at last fainted in the hall of her house. In the midst of the business of the senate-house Brutus heard that his wife was dying.

Porcia was not with her husband during the

campaigns that ended at Philippi, but remained in Rome.   She is said to have killed herself by swallowing the live coals from a brazier, when her friends kept from her all the means of self-destruction.   This story is scarcely credible ; possibly it means that she suffocated herself with the fumes of charcoal.   That she should commit suicide suited all the traditions of her life.

CHAPTER XIII.

A GOVERNOR IN HIS PROVINCE.

It was usual for a Roman statesman, after filling the office of prætor or consul, to undertake for a year or more the government of one of the provinces. These appointments were indeed the prizes of the profession of politics. The new governor had a magnificent outfit from the treasury. We hear of as much as one hundred and fifty thousand pounds having been allowed for this purpose. Out of this something might easily be economized. Indeed we hear of one governor who left the whole of his allowance put out at interest in Rome. And in the province itself splendid gains might be, and indeed commonly were, got. Even Cicero, who, if we may trust his

own account of his proceedings, was exception-
ally just, and not only just, but even generous in
his dealings with the provincials, made, as we
have seen, the very handsome profit of twenty
thousand pounds out of a year of office.
Verres, who, on the other hand, was excep-
tionally rapacious, made three hundred and
fifty thousand pounds in three years, besides
collecting works of art of incalculable value.
But the honors and profits to which most of
his contemporaries looked forward with eagerness did not attract Cicero. He did not care
to be absent from the center of political life,
and felt himself to be at once superior to and
unfitted for the pettier affairs of a provincial
government.

He had successfully avoided the appointment
after his prætorship and again after his consulship. But the time came when it was forced
upon him. Pompey in his third consulship
had procured the passing of a law by which it
was provided that all senators who had filled
the office of prætor or consul should cast lots
for the vacant provinces. Cicero had to take
his chance with the rest, and the ballot gave

him Cilicia. This was in B. C. 51, and Cicero was in his fifty-sixth year.

Cilicia was a province of considerable extent, including, as it did, the south-eastern portion of Asia Minor, together with the island of Cyprus. The position of its governor was made more anxious by the neighborhood of Rome's most formidable neighbors, the Parthians, who but two years before had cut to pieces the army of Crassus. Two legions, numbering twelve thousand troops besides auxiliaries, were stationed in the province, having attached to them between two and three thousand cavalry.

Cicero started to take up his appointment on May 1st, accompanied by his brother, who, having served with distinction under Cæsar in Gaul, had resigned his command to act as lieutenant in Cilicia. At Cumæ he received a levee of visitors— a "little Rome," he says. Hortensius was among them, and this though in very feeble health (he died before Cicero's return). "He asked me for my instructions. Every thing else I left with him in general terms, but I begged him especially not to allow, as far as in him lay, the government of

my province to be continued to me into another
year." On the 17th of the month he reached
Tarentum, where he spent three days with
Pompey. He found him " ready to defend the
State from the dangers that we dread." The
shadows of the civil war, which was to break
out in the year after Cicero's return, were
already gathering. At Brundisium, the port
of embarkation for the East, he was detained
partly by indisposition, partly by having to
wait for one of his officials for nearly a
fortnight. He reached Actium, in north-
western Greece, on the 15th of June. He
would have liked to proceed thence by land,
being, as he tells us, a bad sailor, and having
in view the rounding of the formidable pro-
montory Leucate ; but there was a difficulty
about his retinue, without which he could not
maintain the state which became a governor
en route for his province. Eleven more days
brought him to Athens. " So far," he writes
from this place, "no expenditure of public or
private money has been made on me or any
of my retinue. I have convinced all my people
that they must do their best for my character.

So far all has gone admirably. The thing has been noticed, and is greatly praised by the Greeks." "Athens," he writes again, "delighted me much ; the city with all its beauty, the great affection felt for you" (he is writing, it will be remembered, to Atticus, an old resident), "and the good feeling towards myself, much more, too, its philosophical studies." He was able before he left to do the people a service, rescuing from the hands of the builder the house of Epicurus, which the council of Areopagus, with as little feeling for antiquity as a modern town council, had doomed. Then he went on his way, grumbling at the hardships of a sea voyage in July, at the violence of the winds, at the smallness of the local vessels. He reached Ephesus on July 22nd, without being sea-sick, as he is careful to tell us, and found a vast number of persons who had come to pay their respects to him. All this was pleasant enough, but he was peculiarly anxious to get back to Rome. Rome indeed to the ordinary Roman was—a few singular lovers of the country, as Virgil and Horace, excepted—as Paris is to the Parisian. " Make it absolutely certain," he writes to Atticus, "that I am to be in office for a year only ; that there is not to be even an intercalated month." From Ephesus he journeys, complaining of the hot and dusty roads, to Tralles, and from Tralles, one of the cities of his province, to Laodicea, which he reached July 31st, exactly three months after starting.[1] The distance, directly measured, may be reckoned at something less than a thousand miles.

He seems to have found the province in a deplorable condition. "I staid," he writes, "three days at Laodicea, three again at Apamea, and as many at Synnas, and heard nothing except complaints that they could not pay the poll-tax imposed upon them, that every one's property was sold ; heard, I say, nothing but complaints and groans, and monstrous deeds which seemed to suit not a man but some horrid wild beast. Still it is some alleviation to these unhappy towns that they are put to no expense for me or for any of my followers. I will not receive the fodder which is my legal

[1] Forty-seven days was reckoned a very short time for accomplishing the journey.

due, nor even the wood. Sometimes I have accepted four beds and a roof over my head ; often not even this, preferring to lodge in a tent. The consequence of all this is an incredible concourse of people from town and country anxious to see me. Good heavens ! my very approach seems to make them revive, so completely do the justice, moderation, and clemency of your friend surpass all expectation." It must be allowed that Cicero was not unaccustomed to sound his own praises.

Usury was one of the chief causes of this widespread distress ; and usury, as we have seen, was practiced even by Romans of good repute. We have seen an " honorable man," such as Brutus, exacting an interest of nearly fifty per cent. Pompey was receiving, at what rate of interest we do not know, the enormous sum of nearly one hundred thousand pounds per annum from the tributary king of Cappadocia, and this was less than he was entitled to. Other debtors of this impecunious king could get nothing ; every thing went into Pompey's purse, and the whole country was drained of coin to the very uttermost. In the end, however, Cicero did

manage to get twenty thousand pounds for
Brutus, who was also one of the king's creditors.
We cannot but wonder, if such things went on
under a governor who was really doing his best
to be moderate and just, what was the condition
of the provincials under ordinary rulers.

While Cicero was busy with the condition of
his province, his attention was distracted by
what we may call a Parthian "scare." The
whole army of this people was said to have
crossed the Euphrates under the command of
Pacorus, the king's son. The governor of Syria
had not yet arrived. The second in command
had shut himself up with all his troops in Antioch. Cicero marched into Cappadocia, which
bordered the least defensible side of Cilicia, and
took up a position at the foot of Mount Taurus.
Next came news that Antioch was besieged.
On hearing this he broke up his camp, crossed
the Taurus range by forced marches, and occupied the passes into Syria. The Parthians
raised the siege of Antioch, and suffered con-
siderably at the hands of Cassius during their
retreat.

Though Cicero never crossed swords with the

Parthians, he found or contrived an opportunity of distinguishing himself as a soldier. The independent mountaineers of the border were attacked and defeated ; Cicero was saluted as "Imperator" on the field of battle by his soldiers, and had the satisfaction of occupying for some days the position which Alexander the Great had taken up before the battle of Issus. " And he," says Cicero, who always relates his military achievements with something like a smile on his face, " was a somewhat better general than either you or I." He next turned his arms against the Free Cilicians, investing in regular form with trenches, earthworks, catapults, and all the regular machinery of a siege, their strong-hold Pindenissum. At the end of forty-seven days the place surrendered. Cicero gave the plunder of the place to his host, reserving the horses only for public purposes. A considerable sum was realized by the sale of slaves. " Who in the world are these Pindenissi ? who are they ?" you will say. " I never heard the name." " Well, what can I do ? I can't make Cilicia another Ætolia, or another Macedonia." The campaign was concluded about the middle of December, and the governor, handing over the army to his brother, made his way to Laodicea. From this place he writes to Atticus in language that seems to us self-glorious and boastful, but still has a ring of honesty about it. " I left Tarsus for Asia (the Roman province so called) on June 5th, followed by such admiration as I cannot express from the cities of Cilicia, and especially from the people of Tarsus. When I had crossed the Taurus there was a marvelous eagerness to see me in Asia as far as my districts extended. During six months of my government they had not received a single requisition from me, had not had a single person quartered upon them. Year after year before my time this part of the year had been turned to profit in this way. The wealthy cities used to pay large sums of money not to have to find winter quarters for the soldiers. Cyprus paid more than £48,000 on this account; and from this island—I say it without exaggeration and in sober truth—not a single coin was levied while I was in power. In return for these benefits, benefits at which they are simply astonished, I will not allow any but verbal honors to be voted to me. Statues, temples, chariots of bronze, I forbid. In nothing do I make myself a trouble to the cities, though it is possible I do so to you, while I thus proclaim my own praises. Bear with me, if you love me. This is the rule which you would have had me follow. My journey through Asia had such results that even the famine—and than famine there is no more deplorable calamity—which then prevailed in the country (there had been no harvest) was an event for me to desire ; for wherever I journeyed, without force, without the help of law, without reproaches, but my simple influence and expostulations, I prevailed upon the Greeks and Roman citizens, who had secreted the corn, to engage to convey a large quantity to the various tribes." He writes again : " I see that you are pleased with my moderation and self-restraint. You would be much more pleased if you were here. At the sessions which I held at Laodicea for all my districts, excepting Cilicia, from February 15th to May 1st, I effected a really marvelous work. Many cities were entirely freed from their debts, many greatly relieved, and all of them enjoying their own laws and courts, and so obtaining self-government received new life. There were two ways in which I gave them the opportunity of either throwing off or greatly lightening the burden of debt. First : they have been put to no expense under my rule—I do not exagger-ate ; I positively say that they have not to spend a farthing. Then again : the cities had been atrociously robbed by their own Greek magistrates. I myself questioned the men who had borne office during the last ten years. They confessed and, without being publicly disgraced, made restitution. In other respects my government, without being wanting in address, is marked by clemency and courtesy. There is none of the difficulty, so usual in the provinces, of approaching me ; no introduction by a chamberlain. Before dawn I am on foot in my house, as I used to be in old days when I was a candidate for office. This is a great matter here and a popular, and to myself, from my old practice in it, has not yet been trouble-some."

He had other less serious cares. One Cælius, who was good enough to keep him informed of what was happening at Rome, and whom we find filling his letters with an amusing mixture of politics, scandal, and gossip, makes a modest request for some panthers, which the governor of so wild a country would doubtless have no difficulty in procuring for him. He was a candidate for the office of ædile, and wanted the beasts for the show which he would have to exhibit. Cicero must not forget to look after them as soon as he hears of the election. " In nearly all my letters I have written to you about the panthers. It will be discreditable to you, that Patiscus should have sent to Curio ten panthers, and you not many times more. These ten Curio gave me, and ten others from Africa. If you will only remember to send for hunters from Cibyra, and also send letters to Pamphylia (for there, I understand, more are taken than elsewhere), you will succeed. I do beseech you look after this matter. You have only to give the orders. I have provided people to keep and transport the animals when once taken." The governor would not hear of imposing the charge of capturing the panthers on the hunters of the province. Still he would do his best

to oblige his friend. " The matter of the panthers is being diligently attended to by the
persons who are accustomed to hunt them ;
but there is a strange scarcity of them, and the
few that there are complain grievously, saying
that they are the only creatures in my province that are persecuted."

From Laodicea Cicero returned to Tarsus,
the capital of his province, wound up the
affairs of his government, appointed an acting
governor, and started homewards early in
August. On his way he paid a visit to
Rhodes, wishing to show to his son and nephew (they had accompanied him to his government) the famous school of eloquence in
which he had himself studied. Here he heard
with much regret of the death of Hortensius.
He had seen the great orator's son at Laodicea,
where he was amusing himself in the disrep-
utable company of some gladiators, and had
asked him to dinner, for his father's sake, he
says. His stay at Rhodes was probably of
some duration, for he did not reach Ephesus
till the first of October. A tedious passage of
fourteen days brought him to Athens. On his

journey westwards Tiro, his confidential servant, was seized with illness, and had to be left
behind at Patræ. Tiro was a slave, though
afterwards set free by his master ; but he was
a man of great and varied accomplishments,
and Cicero writes to him as he might to the
very dearest of his friends. There is nothing
stranger in all that we know of " Roman Life"
than the presence in it of such men as Tiro.
Nor is there any thing, we might even venture
to say, quite like it elsewhere in the whole history of the world. Now and then, in the days
when slavery still existed in the Southern
States of America, mulatto and quadroon slaves
might have been found who in point of appearance and accomplishments were scarcely
different from their owners. But there was
always a taint, or what was reckoned as a taint,
of negro blood in the men and women so situated. In Rome it must have been common
to see men, possibly better born (for Greek
might even be counted better than Roman
descent), and probably better educated than
their masters, who had absolutely no rights as
human beings, and could be tortured or killed

just as cruelty or caprice might suggest. To Tiro, man of culture and acute intellect as he was, there must have been an unspeakable bitterness in the thought of servitude, even under a master so kindly and affectionate as Cicero. One shudders to think what the feelings of such a man must have been when he was the chattel of a Verres, a Clodius, or a Catiline. It is pleasant to turn away from the thought, which is the very darkest perhaps in the repulsive subject of Roman slavery, to observe the sympathy and tenderness which Cicero shows to the sick man from whom he has been reluctantly compelled to part. The letters to Tiro fill one of the sixteen books of " Letters to Friends." They are twenty-seven in number, or rather twenty-six, as the sixteenth of the series contains the congratulations and thanks which Quintus Cicero addresses to his brother on receiving the news that Tiro has received his freedom. " As to Tiro," he writes, " I protest, as I wish to see you, my dear Marcus, and my own son, and yours, and my dear Tullia, that you have done a thing that pleased me exceedingly in making a man who certainly was far above his mean condition a friend rather than a servant. Believe me, when I read your letters and his, I fairly leaped for joy; I both thank and congratulate you. If the fidelity of my Statius gives me so much pleasure,[1] how valuable in Tiro must be this same good quality with the additional and even superior advantages of culture, wit, and politeness? I have many very good reasons for loving you; and now there is this that you have told me, as indeed you were bound to tell me, this excellent piece of news. I saw all your heart in your letter."

Cicero's letters to the invalid are at first very frequent. One is dated on the third, another on the fifth, and a third on the seventh of November; and on the eighth of the month there are no fewer than three, the first of them apparently in answer to a letter from Tiro. " I am variously affected by your letter—much troubled by the first page, a little comforted by the second. The result is that I now say, without hesitation, till you are quite strong, do not trust yourself to travel either by land or

[1] See page 277.

sea. I shall see you as soon as I wish if I see you quite restored." He goes on to criticise the doctor's prescriptions. Soup was not the right thing to give to a dyspeptic patient. Tiro is not to spare any expense. Another fee to the doctor might make him more attentive. In another letter he regrets that the invalid had felt himself compelled to accept an invitation to a concert, and tells him that he had left a horse and mule for him at Brundisium. Then, after a brief notice of public affairs, he returns to the question of the voyage. " I must again ask you not to be rash in your traveling. Sailors, I observe, make too much haste to increase their profits. Be cautious, my dear Tiro. You have a wide and dangerous sea to traverse. If you can, come with Mescinius. He is wont to be careful in his voyages. If not with him, come with a person of distinction, who will have influence with the captain." In another letter he tells Tiro that he must revive his love of letters and learning. The physician thought that his mind was ill at ease ; for this the best remedy was occupation. In another he writes : " I have received your letter with its shaky handwriting; no wonder, indeed, seeing how serious has been your illness. I send you Ægypta (probably a superior slave) to wait upon you, and a cook with him." Cicero could not have shown more affectionate care of a sick son.

Tiro is said to have written a life of his master. And we certainly owe to his care the preservation of his correspondence. His weak health did not prevent him from living to the age of a hundred and three.

Cicero pursued his homeward journey by slow stages, and it was not till November 25th that he reached Italy. His mind was distracted between two anxieties—the danger of civil war, which he perceived to be daily growing more imminent, and an anxious desire to have his military successes over the Cilician mountaineers rewarded by the distinction of a triumph. The honor of a public thanksgiving had already been voted to him; Cato, who opposed it on principle, having given him offense by so doing. A triumph was less easy to obtain, and indeed it seems to show a certain weakness in Cicero that he should have sought

to obtain it for exploits of so very moderate a
kind. However, he landed at Brundisium as
a formal claimant for the honor. His lictors
had their fasces (bundles of rods inclosing
an ax) wreathed with bay leaves, as was
the custom with the victorious general who
hoped to obtain this distinction. Pompey,
with whom he had a long interview, encouraged
him to hope for it, and promised his support.
It was not till January 4th that he reached the
capital. The look of affairs was growing
darker and darker, but he still clung to the
hopes of a triumph, and would not dismiss his
lictors with their ornaments, though he was
heartily wearied of their company. Things
went so far that a proposition was actually
made in the Senate that the triumph should be
granted ; but the matter was postponed at the
suggestion of one of the consuls, anxious,
Cicero thinks, to make his own services more
appreciated when the time should come.
Before the end of January he seems to have
given up his hopes. In a few more days he
was fairly embarked on the tide of civil war.

CHAPTER XIV.

ATTICUS.

THE name of Atticus has been mentioned more
than once in the preceding chapters as a correspondent of Cicero. We have indeed more
than five hundred letters addressed to him,
extending over a period of almost five-and-
twenty years. There are frequent intervals of
silence—not a single letter, for instance, belongs
to the year of the consulship, the reason being
that both the correspondents were in Rome.
Sometimes, especially in the later years, they
follow each other very closely. The last was
written about a year before Cicero's death.

Atticus was one of those rare characters who
contrive to live at peace with all men. The
times were troublous beyond all measure ;
he had wealth and position ; he kept up close
friendship with men who were in the very

thickest of the fight; he was ever ready with his sympathy and help for those who were vanquished; and yet he contrived to arouse no enmities; and after a life-long peace, interrupted only by one or two temporary alarms, died in a good old age.

Atticus was of what we should call a gentleman's family, and belonged by inheritance to the democratic party. But he early resolved to stand aloof from politics, and took an effectual means of carrying out his purpose by taking up his residence at Athens. With characteristic prudence he transferred the greater part of his property to investments in Greece. At Athens he became exceedingly popular. He lent money at easy rates to the municipality, and made liberal distributions of corn, giving as much as a bushel and a half to every needy citizen. He spoke Greek and Latin with equal ease and eloquence; and had, we are told, an unsurpassed gift for reciting poetry. Sulla, who, for all his savagery, had a cultivated taste, was charmed with the young man, and would have taken him in his train. " I beseech you," replied Atticus, " don't take me to fight against those in whose company, but that I left Italy, I might be fighting against you." After a residence of twenty-three years he returned to Rome, in the very year of Cicero's consulship. At Rome he stood as much aloof from the turmoil of civil strife as he had stood at Athens. Office of every kind he steadily refused; he was under no obligations to any man, and therefore was not thought ungrateful by any. The partisans of Cæsar and of Pompey were content to receive help from his purse, and to see him resolutely neutral. He refused to join in a project of presenting what we should call a testimonial to the murderers of Cæsar on behalf of the order of the knights; but he did not hesitate to relieve the necessities of the most conspicuous of them with a present of between three and four thousand pounds. When Antony was outlawed he protected his family; and Antony in return secured his life and property amidst the horrors of the second Proscription.

His biographer, Cornelius Nepos, has much to say of his moderation and temperate habits of life. He had no sumptuous country-house in the suburbs or at the sea-coast, but two farm-houses. He possessed, however, what seems to have been a very fine house (perhaps we should call it " castle," for Cicero speaks of it as a place capable of defense) in Epirus. It contained among other things a gallery of statues. A love of letters was one of his chief characteristics. His guests were not entertained with the performances of hired singers, but with readings from authors of repute. He had collected, indeed, a very large library. All his slaves, down to the very meanest, were well educated, and he employed them to make copies.

Atticus married somewhat late in life. His only daughter was the first wife of Agrippa, the minister of Augustus, and his granddaughter was married to Tiberius. Both of these ladies were divorced to make room for a consort of higher rank, who, curiously enough, was in both cases Julia, the infamous daughter of Augustus. Both, we may well believe, were regretted by their husbands.

Atticus died at the age of seventy-seven. He was afflicted with a disease which he believed to be incurable, and shortened his days by voluntary starvation.

It was to this correspondent, then, that Cicero confided for about a quarter of a century his cares and his wants. The two had been schoolfellows, and had probably renewed their acquaintance when Cicero visited Greece in search of health. Afterwards there came to be a family connection between them, Atticus' sister, Pomponia, marrying Cicero's younger brother, Quintus, not much, we gather from the letters, to the happiness of either of them. Cicero could not have had a better confidant. He was full of sympathy, and ready with his help; and he was at the same time sagacious and prudent in no common degree, an excellent man of business, and, thanks to the admirable coolness which enabled him to stand outside the turmoil of politics, an equally excellent adviser in politics.

One frequent subject of Cicero's letters to his friend is money. I may perhaps express the relation between the two by saying that Atticus was Cicero's banker, though the phrase must not be taken too literally. He did not

DYING GLADIATOR.

habitually receive and pay money on Cicero's account, but he did so on occasions ; and he was constantly in the habit of making advances, though probably without interest, when temporary embarrassments, not infrequent, as we may gather from the letters, called for them. Atticus was himself a wealthy man. Like his contemporaries generally, he made an income by money-lending, and possibly, for the point is not quite clear, by letting out gladiators for hire. His biographer happens to give us the precise figure of his property. His words do not indeed expressly state whether the sum that he mentions means capital or income. I am inclined to think that it is the latter. If this be so, he had in early life an income of something less than eighteen thousand pounds, and afterwards nearly ninety thousand pounds.

I may take this occasion to say something about Cicero's property, a matter which is, in its way, a rather perplexing question. In the case of a famous advocate among ourselves there would be no difficulty in understanding that he should have acquired a great fortune. But the

Roman law strictly forbade an advocate to receive any payment from his clients. The practice of old times, when the great noble pleaded for the life or property of his humbler defendants, and was repaid by their attachment and support, still existed in theory. It exists indeed to this day, and accounts for the fact that a barrister among ourselves has no *legal* means of recovering his fees. But a practice of paying counsel had begun to grow up. Some of Cicero's contemporaries certainly received a large remuneration for their services. Cicero himself always claims to have kept his hands clean in this respect, and as his enemies never brought any charge of this kind against him, his statement may very well be accepted. We have, then, to look for other sources of income. His patrimony was considerable. It included, as we have seen, an estate at Arpinum and a house in Rome. And then he had numerous legacies. This is a source of income which is almost strange to our modern ways of acting and thinking. It seldom happens among us that a man of property leaves any thing outside the circle of his family. Sometimes an intimate friend will receive a legacy. But instances of money bequeathed to a statesman in recognition of his services, or a literary man in recognition of his eminence, are exceedingly rare. In Rome they were very common. Cicero declares, giving it as a proof of the way in which he had been appreciated by his fellow-citizens, that he had received two hundred thousand pounds in legacies. This was in the last year of his life. This does something to help us out of our difficulty. Only we must remember that it could hardly have been till somewhat late in his career that these recognitions of his services to the State and to his friends began to fall in. He made about twenty thousand pounds out of his year's government of his province, but it is probable that this money was lost. Then, again, he was elected into the College of Augurs (this was in his fifty-fourth year). These religious colleges were very rich. Their banquets were proverbial for their splendor. Whether the individual members derived any benefit from their revenues we do not know. We often find him complaining of debt ; but he always speaks of it as a temporary inconvenience rather than as a permanent burden. It does not oppress him ; he can always find spirits enough to laugh at it. When he buys his great town mansion on the Palatine Hill (it had belonged to the wealthy Crassus), for thirty thousand pounds, he says, " I now owe so much that I should be glad to conspire if any body would accept me as an accomplice." But this is not the way in which a man who did not see his way out of his difficulties would speak.

Domestic affairs furnish a frequent topic. He gives accounts of the health of his wife ; he announces the birth of his children. In after years he sends the news when his daughter is betrothed and when she is married, and tells of the doings and prospects of his son. He has also a good deal to say about his brother's household, which, as I have said before, was not very happy. Here is a scene of their domestic life. "When I reached Arpinum, my brother came to me. First we had much talk about you ; afterwards we came to the subject which you and I had discussed at

Tusculum. I never saw any thing so gentle, so kind as my brother was in speaking of your sister. If there had been any ground for their disagreement, there was nothing to notice. So much for that day. On the morrow we left for Arpinum. Quintus had to remain in the Retreat ; I was going to stay at Aquinum. Still we lunched at the Retreat (you know the place). When we arrived Quintus said in the politest way, ' Pomponia, ask the ladies in ; I will call the servants,' Nothing could—so at least I thought—have been more pleasantly said, not only as far as words go, but in tone and look. However, she answered before us all, ' I am myself but a stranger here.' This, I fancy, was because Statius had gone on in advance to see after the lunch. ' See,' said Quintus, ' this is what I have to put up with every day.' Perhaps you will say, ' What was there in this ?' It was really serious, so serious as to disturb me much, so unreasonably, so angrily did she speak and look. I did not show it, but I was greatly vexed. We all sat down to table, all, that is, but her. However, Quintus sent her something from the table. She refused it.

Not to make a long story of it, no one could have been more gentle than my brother, and no one more exasperating than your sister—in my judgment at least, and I pass by many other things which offended me more than they did Quintus. I went on to Aquinum." (The lady's behavior was all the more blameworthy because her husband was on his way to a remote province.) "Quintus remained at the Retreat. The next day he joined me at Arpinum. Your sister, he told me, would have nothing to do with him, and up to the moment of her departure was just in the same mood in which I had seen her."

Another specimen of letters touching on a more agreeable topic may interest my readers. It is a hearty invitation.

"To my delight, Cincius" (he was Atticus' agent) "came to me between daylight on January 30th, with the news that you were in Italy. He was sending, he said, messengers to you. I did not like them to go without a letter from me, not that I had any thing to write to you, especially when you were so close, but that I wished you to understand with what delight I

anticipate your coming. . . . The day you arrive
come to my house with all your party. You
will find that Tyrannio" (a Greek man of letters)
"has arranged my books marvelously well.
What remains of them is much more satisfactory than I thought.[1] I should be glad if you
would send me two of your library clerks, for
Tullius to employ as binders and helpers in
general ; give some orders too to take some
parchment for indices. All this, however, if it
suits your convenience. Any how, come yourself
and bring Pilia[2] with you. That is but right,
Tullia too wishes it."

[1] They had suffered with the rest of Cicero's property
at the time of his exile.

[2] Pilia was the lady to whom Atticus was engaged

CHAPTER XV.

ANTONY AND AUGUSTUS.

THERE were some things in which Mark Antony resembled Cæsar. At the time it seemed probable that he would play the same part, and even climb to the same height of power. He failed in the end because he wanted the power of managing others, and, still more, of controlling himself. He came of a good stock. His grandfather had been one of the greatest orators of his day, his father was a kindly, generous man, his mother a kinswoman of Cæsar, a matron of the best Roman type. But he seemed little likely to do credit to his belongings. His riotous life became conspicuous even in a city where extravagance and vice were only too common, and his debts, though not so enormous as Cæsar's, were greater, says Plutarch, than became his youth, for they

MARCUS ANTONIUS.

amounted to about fifty thousand pounds. He was taken away from these dissipations by military service in the East, and he rapidly acquired considerable reputation as a soldier. Here is the picture that Plutarch draws of him :

There was something noble and dignified in his appearance. His handsome beard, his broad forehead, his aquiline nose, gave him a manly look that resembled the familiar statues and pictures of Hercules. There was indeed a legend that the Antonii were descended from a son of Hercules ; and this he was anxious to support by his appearance and dress. Whenever he appeared in public he had his tunic gired up to the hip, carried a great sword at his side, and wore a rough cloak of Cilician hair. The habits too that seemed vulgar to others— his boastfulness, his coarse humor, his drinking bouts, the way he had of eating in public, taking his meals as he stood from the soldiers' tables—had an astonishing effect in making him popular with the soldiers. His bounty too, the help which he gave with a liberal hand to comrades and friends, made his way to power easy. On one occasion he directed that a present of three thousand pounds should be given to a friend. His steward, aghast at the magnitude of the sum, thought to bring it home to his master's mind by putting the actual coin on a table. " What is this ? " said Antony, as he happened to pass by. " The money you bade me pay over," was the man's reply. " Why, I had thought it would be ten times as much as this. This is but a trifle. Add to it as much more."

When the civil war broke out, Antony joined the party of Cæsar, who, knowing his popularity with the troops, made him his second in command. He did good service at Pharsalia, and while his chief went on to Egypt, returned to Rome as his representative. There were afterwards differences between the two ; Cæsar was offended at the open scandal of Antony's manners and found him a troublesome adherent ; Antony conceived himself to be insufficiently rewarded for his services, especially when he was called upon to pay for Pompey's confiscated property, which he had bought. Their close alliance, however, had been renewed before Cæsar's death. That event made him the first man in Rome. The chief instrument of his power was a strange one ; the Senate, seeing that the people of Rome loved and admired the dead man, passed a resolution that all the wishes which Cæsar had left in writing should have the force of law—and Antony had the custody of his papers. People laughed, and called the documents " Letters from the Styx." There was the gravest suspicion that many of them were forged. But for a time they were a very powerful machinery for effecting his purpose.

Then came a check. Cæsar's nephew and heir, Octavius, arrived at Rome. Born in the year of Cicero's consulship, he was little more than nineteen ; but in prudence, statecraft, and knowledge of the world he was fully grown. In his twelfth year he had delivered the funeral oration over his grandmother Julia. After winning some distinction as a soldier in Spain, he had returned at his uncle's bidding to Apollonia, a town of the eastern coast of the Adriatic, where he studied letters and philosophy under Greek teachers. Here he had received the title of "Master of the Horse," an honor which gave him the rank next to the Dictator himself. He came to Rome with the purpose, as he declared, of claiming his inheritance and avenging his uncle's death. But he knew how to abide his time. He kept on terms with Antony, who had usurped his position and appropriated his inheritance, and he was friendly, if not with the actual murderers of Cæsar, yet certainly with Cicero, who made no secret of having approved their deed.

For Cicero also had now returned to public life. For some time past, both before Cæsar's death and after it, he had devoted himself to literature.[1] Now there seemed to him a chance that something might yet be done for the republic, and he returned to Rome, which he reached on the last day of August. The next day there was a meeting of the Senate, at which Antony was to propose certain honors to Cæsar. Cicero, wearied, or affecting to be wearied, by his journey, was absent, and was fiercely attacked by Antony, who threatened to send workmen to dig him out of his house.

---

[1] To the years 46–44 belong nearly all his treatises on rhetoric and philosophy.

The next day Cicero was in his place, Antony being absent, and made a dignified defense of his conduct, and criticised with some severity the proceedings of his assailant. Still so far there was no irreconcilable breach between the two men. "Change your course," says the orator, "I beseech you : think of those who have gone before, and so steer the course of the Commonwealth that your countrymen may rejoice that you were born. Without this no man can be happy or famous." He still believed, or professed to believe, that Antony was capable of patriotism. If he had any hopes of peace, these were soon to be crushed. After a fortnight or more spent in preparation, assisted, we are told, by a professional teacher of eloquence, Antony came down to the Senate and delivered a savage invective against Cicero. The object of his attack was again absent. He had wished to attend the meeting, but his friends hindered him, fearing, not without reason, actual violence from the armed attendants whom Antony was accustomed to bring into the senate-house.

The attack was answered in the famous

oration which is called the second Philippic.[1]
If I could transcribe this speech (which, for
other reasons besides its length, I cannot do)
it would give us a strange picture of "Roman
Life." It is almost incredible that a man so
shameless and so vile should have been the
greatest power in a state still nominally free.
I shall give one extract from it. Cicero has
been speaking of Antony's purchase of Pompey's confiscated property. "He was wild with
joy, like a character in a farce; a beggar one
day, a millionaire the next. But, as some
writer says, 'Ill gotten, ill kept.' It is beyond
belief, it is an absolute miracle, how he squan-
dered this vast property—in a few months do
I say?—no, in a few days. There was a great
cellar of wine, a very great quantity of excellent
plate, costly stuffs, plenty of elegant and even
splendid furniture, just as one might expect in
a man who was affluent without being luxurious. And of all this within a few days there

[1] The orations against Antony—there are fourteen of
them—are called "Philippics," a name transferred to them
from the great speeches in which Demosthenes attacked
Philip of Macedon. The name seems to have been in
common use in Juvenal's time (*circa* 110 A.D.)

was left nothing. Was there ever a Charybdis so devouring? A Charybdis, do I say? no—if there ever was such a thing, it was but a single animal. Good heavens! I can scarcely believe that the whole ocean could have swallowed up so quickly possessions so numerous, so scattered, and lying at places so distant. Nothing was locked up, nothing sealed, nothing catalogued. Whole store-rooms were made a present of to the vilest creatures. Actors and actresses of burlesque were busy each with plunder of their own. The mansion was full of dice players and drunkards. There was drinking from morning to night, and that in many places. His losses at dice (for even he is not always lucky) kept mounting up. In the chambers of slaves you might see on the beds the purple coverlets which had belonged to the great Pompey. No wonder that all this wealth was spent so quickly. Reckless men so abandoned might well have speedily devoured, not only the patrimony of a single citizen, however ample—and ample it was—but whole cities and kingdoms."

The speech was never delivered but circulated in writing. Toward the end of 44, Antony, who found the army deserting him for the young Octavius, left Rome, and hastened into northern Italy, to attack Decimus Brutus. Brutus was not strong enough to venture on a battle with him, and shut himself up in Mutina. Cicero continued to take the leading part in affairs at Rome, delivering the third and fourth Philippics in December, 44, and the ten others during the five months of the following year. The fourteenth was spoken in the Senate, when the fortunes of the falling republic seem to have revived. A great battle had been fought at Mutina, in which Antony had been completely defeated; and Cicero proposed thanks to the commanders and troops, and honors to those who had fallen.

The joy with which these tidings had been received was but very brief. Of the three generals named in the vote of thanks the two who had been loyal to the republic were dead; the third, the young Octavius, had found the opportunity for which he had been waiting of betraying it. The soldiers were ready to do his bidding, and he resolved to seize by their

OCTAVIUS CÆSAR AUGUSTUS.

help the inheritance of power which his uncle had left him. Antony had fled across the Alps, and had been received by Lepidus, who was in command of a large army in that province. Lepidus resolved to play the part which Crassus had played sixteen years before. He brought about a reconciliation between Octavius and Antony, as Crassus had reconciled Pompey and Cæsar, and was himself admitted as a third into their alliance. Thus was formed the Second Triumvirate.

The three chiefs who had agreed to divide the Roman world between them met on a little island near Bononia (the modern Bonogna) and discussed their plans. Three days were given to their consultations, the chief subject being the catalogue of enemies, public and private, who were to be destroyed. Each had a list of his own ; and on Antony's the first name was Cicero. Lepidus assented, as he was ready to assent to all the demands of his more resolute colleagues ; but the young Octavius is said to have long resisted, and to have given way only on the last day. A list of between two and three thousand names of senators and knights was drawn up. Seventeen were singled out for instant execution, and among these seventeen was Cicero. He was staying at his home in Tusculum with his brother Quintus when the news reached him. His first impulse was to make for the sea-coast. If he could reach Macedonia, where Brutus had a powerful army, he would, for a time at least, be safe. The two brothers started. But Quintus had little or nothing with him, and was obliged to go home to fetch some money. Cicero, who was himself but ill provided, pursued his journey alone. Reaching the coast, he embarked. When it came to the point of leaving Italy his resolution failed him. He had always felt the greatest aversion for camp life. He had had an odious experience of it when Pompey was struggling with Cæsar for the mastery. He would sooner die, he thought, than make trial of it again. He landed, and traveled twelve miles towards Rome. Some afterwards said that he still cherished hopes of being protected by Antony ; others that it was his purpose to make his way into the house of Octavius and kill himself on his hearth, cursing him with his last breath, but that he was deterred by the fear of being seized and tortured. Any how, he turned back, and allowed his slaves to take him to Capua. The plan of taking refuge with Brutus was probably urged upon him by his companions, who felt that this gave the only chance of their own escape. Again he embarked, and again he landed. Plutarch tells a strange story of a flock of ravens that settled on the yardarms of his ship while he was on board, and on the windows of the villa in which he passed the night. One bird, he says, flew upon his couch and pecked at the cloak in which he had wrapped himself. His slaves reproached themselves at allowing a master, whom the very animals were thus seeking to help, to perish before their eyes. Almost by main force they put him into his litter and carried him toward the coast. Antony's soldiers now reached the villa, the officer in command being an old client whom Cicero had successfully defended on a charge of murder. They found the doors shut and burst them open. The inmates denied all knowledge of their master's movements, till a young Greek, one of his brother's freedmen, whom

Cicero had taken a pleasure in teaching, showed the officer the litter which was being carried through the shrubbery of the villa to the sea. Taking with him some of his men, he hastened to follow. Cicero, hearing their steps, bade the bearers set the litter on the ground. He looked out, and stroking his chin with his left hand, as his habit was, looked steadfastly at the murderers. His face was pale and worn with care. The officer struck him on the neck with his sword, some of the rough soldiers turning away while the deed was done. The head and hands were cut off by order of Antony, and nailed up in the Forum.

Many years afterwards the Emperor Augustus (the Octavius of this chapter), coming unexpectedly upon one of his grandsons, saw the lad seek to hide in his robe a volume which he had been reading. He took it, and found it to be one of the treatises of Cicero. He returned it with words which I would here repeat ; " He was a good man and a lover of his country."

THE END.